DATE DUE

			PRINTED IN U.S.A.

Post-Impressionism

GREAT ARTISTS OF THE WESTERN WORLD

Post-Impressionism

Paul Cézanne

———❦———

Paul Gauguin

———❦———

Vincent van Gogh

———❦———

Georges Seurat

MARSHALL CAVENDISH · LONDON · NEW YORK · SYDNEY

Staff Credits

Editors	Clive Gregory LLB Sue Lyon BA (Honours)	**Picture Researchers**	Vanessa Fletcher BA (Honours) Flavia Howard BA (Honours) Jessica Johnson BA
Art Editors	Chris Legee BFA Kate Sprawson BA (Honours) Keith Vollans LSIAD	**Production Controllers**	Tom Helsby Alan Stewart BSc
Deputy Editor	John Kirkwood BSc (Honours)	**Secretary**	Lynn Smail
Sub-editors	Caroline Bugler BA (Honours), MA Sue Churchill BA (Honours) Alison Cole BA, MPhil Jenny Mohammadi Nigel Rodgers BA (Honours), MA Penny Smith Will Steeds BA (Honours), MA	**Editorial Director**	Maggi McCormick
		Publishing Manager	Robert Paulley BSc
		Managing Editor	Alan Ross BA (Honours)
Designers	Stuart John Julie Stanniland	**Consultant and Authenticator**	Sharon Fermor BA (Honours) Lecturer in the Extra-Mural Department of London University and Lecturer in Art History at Sussex University

Reference Edition Published 1988

Published by Marshall Cavendish Corporation
147 West Merrick Road
Freeport, Long Island
N.Y. 11520

Typeset by Litho Link Ltd., Welshpool
Printed and Bound by Dai Nippon
Printing Co., Hong Kong Ltd.

Library of Congress Cataloging-in-Publication Data

Main entry under title:

Great Artists of the Western World II.

Includes index.
1. Artists – Biography. I. Marshall Cavendish Corporation.
N40.G774 1988   709'.2'2 [B]   88–4317
ISBN 0–86307–900–8 (set)

ISBN 0–86307–900–8 (set)
0–86307–758–7 (vol)

Preface

Looking at pictures can be one of the greatest pleasures that life has to offer. Note, however, those two words 'can be'; all too many of us remember all too clearly those grim afternoons of childhood when we were dragged, bored to tears and complaining bitterly, through room after room of Italian primitives by well-meaning relations or tight-lipped teachers. It was enough to put one off pictures for life – which, for some of us, was exactly what it did.

For if gallery-going is to be the fun it should be, certain conditions must be fulfilled. First, the pictures we are to see must be good pictures. Not necessarily great pictures – even a few of these can be daunting, while too many at a time may prove dangerously indigestible. But they must be well-painted, by good artists who know precisely both the effect they want to achieve and how best to achieve it. Second, we must limit ourselves as to quantity. Three rooms – four at the most – of the average gallery are more than enough for one day, and for best results we should always leave while we are still fresh, well before satiety sets in. Now I am well aware that this is a counsel of perfection: sometimes, in the case of a visiting exhibition or, perhaps, when we are in a foreign city with only a day to spare, we shall have no choice but to grit our teeth and stagger on to the end. But we shall not enjoy ourselves quite so much, nor will the pictures remain so long or so clearly in our memory.

The third condition is all-important: we must know something about the painters whose work we are looking at. And this is where this magnificent series of volumes – one of which you now hold in your hands – can make all the difference. No painting is an island: it must, if it is to be worth a moment's attention, express something of the personality of its painter. And that painter, however individual a genius, cannot but reflect the country, style and period, together with the views and attitudes of the people among whom he or she was born and bred. Even a superficial understanding of these things will illuminate a painting for us far better than any number of spotlights, and if in addition we have learnt something about the artist as a person – life and loves, character and beliefs, friends and patrons, and the places to which he or she travelled – the interest and pleasure that the work will give us will be multiplied a hundredfold.

Great Artists of the Western World will provide you with just such an insight into the life

and work of some of the outstanding painters of Europe and America. The text is informative without ever becoming dry or academic, not limiting itself to the usual potted biographies but forever branching out into the contemporary world outside and beyond workshop or studio. The illustrations, in colour throughout, have been dispensed in almost reckless profusion. For those who, like me, revel in playing the Attribution Game – the object of which is to guess the painter of each picture before allowing one's eye to drop to the label – the little sections on 'Trademarks' are a particularly happy feature; but every aficionado will have particular preferences, and I doubt whether there is an art historian alive, however distinguished, who would not find some fascinating nugget of previously unknown information among the pages that follow.

This series, however, is not intended for art historians. It is designed for ordinary people like you and me – and for our older children – who are fully aware that the art galleries of the world constitute a virtually bottomless mine of potential enjoyment, and who are determined to extract as much benefit and advantage from it as they possibly can. All the volumes in this collection will enable us to do just that, expanding our knowledge not only of art itself but also of history, religion, mythology, philosophy, fashion, interior decoration, social customs and a thousand other subjects as well. So let us not simply leave them around, flipping idly through a few of their pages once in a while. Let us read them as they deserve to be read – and welcome a new dimension in our lives.

John Julius Norwich is a writer and broadcaster who has written histories of Venice and of Norman Sicily as well as several works on history, art and architecture. He has also made over twenty documentary films for television, including the recent Treasure Houses of Britain series which was widely acclaimed after repeated showings in the United States.

Lord Norwich is Chairman of the Venice in Peril Fund, and member of the Executive Committee of the British National Trust, an independently funded body established for the protection of places of historic interest and natural beauty.

John Julius Norwich

Contents

Introduction

The term 'Post-Impressionism' was coined by the English critic, Roger Fry, for the two important exhibitions of modern French art, which he organized in 1910 and 1912. It was, he recognized, a label of convenience, since it was applied posthumously to a very independent group of artists, who shared no common set of ideals and who worked in quite different styles. Even so, the fact that each of them was concerned to find new ways of progressing beyond the boundaries of Impressionism has proved sufficient to gain general acceptance for the term.

Neo-Impressionism

By the 1880s, at the very time when the Impressionists' work was beginning to reach a wider public, the movement itself was losing impetus. Many painters found that the rejection of moral and intellectual elements in art and the emphasis on transient light effects were too limiting, and some – most notably Degas and Renoir – turned away from the style.

In addition, attempts were made to transform the nature of Impressionism itself, to endow it with a broader scale of values. The most significant of these attempts came from the Neo-Impressionists – also called 'Divisionists' or 'Pointillists' because of their technique – who endorsed the Impressionists' use of pure, unmixed colours, but condemned their intuitive attitudes and sought to employ their methods on a more consistent and rational basis.

This scientific approach was typified by the painstaking researches of Georges Seurat. Visually, Seurat was inspired by Delacroix – the first French artist to make use of optical theories in his paintings – but he elaborated upon these ideas by steeping himself in the writings of Helmholtz about the sensitivity of the eye to certain colour combinations. He also studied the works of Ogden Rood, a professor of physics, whose Modern Chromatics summarized the most recent findings on complementary colours. From these, Rood had produced a circular chart, in which each colour was shown opposite its contrasting tone, and Seurat made extensive use of this as a guide for constructing his compositions.

A final, and more surprising source for Seurat's pointillist style was to be found in his revolutionary chalk drawings (p.113). By rubbing his chalks over rough paper, he discovered that he could break his picture surface down into an area of small dots,

while, at the same time, injecting an air of mystery into the image. This evocative quality was later to inspire the Surrealists to produce their own frottages (rubbings).

The purpose of Seurat's studies was to instil an aesthetic harmony into painting, and it was here that the Neo-Impressionists differed most from their Impressionist colleagues. For, where the latter sought to record a visual sensation, the Pointillists wished instead to create one.

The vogue for Neo-Impressionism was extremely brief. After the exhibiting of La Grande Jatte (pp.122-3), most avant-garde artists adopted the divisionist method eagerly, only to abandon it a year or so later. In part, this was because the technique, if properly applied, was so slow and laborious that it stifled creativity and, in part, it was because the rigidity of the rules proved even more restricting than Impressionism itself.

The true inheritors of Pointillism were the Fauvist painters. Seurat's early death prevented him from contributing to this directly, but his followers, Cross and Signac, were an undoubted influence on the young Matisse during his visits to the south of France.

Art as Abstraction

In some aspects of his art, Seurat was a great traditionalist – namely in his reliance on draughtsmanship and in his insistence on planning his compositions meticulously – while, in other ways, he was very modern. In particular, this modernity showed itself in his taste for depicting his figures as silhouettes, either frontally or in sharp profile (pp.118-19, 122-3, 124-5). This had the effect of stressing the two-dimensional qualities of his paintings and provided a parallel to the flat, linear style of Gauguin. Like Seurat, Gauguin had no interest in lending an impression of weight or volume to his figures. In his case, however, this rejection of naturalism came from a very different source. Gauguin's mature style was forged in Brittany, where it emerged from his meetings with the young artist, Emile Bernard. The latter had developed a technique known as Cloisonnisme – so-called because of its resemblance to cloisonné enamelwork – which was characterized by flat areas of colour and thick, black outlines. Taking this a stage further, Bernard had also abandoned scale and perspective, combining a number of unrelated figures into a single picture.

Basic forms
(above) In Le Chateau
Noir, *Cézanne uses
simplified shapes to convey
the essence, rather than
the precise details, of the
landscape.*

The artists
(from top to bottom)
*Van Gogh at 35; Gauguin
in his early forties;
Cézanne at 40; Seurat at
the age of 23.*

*In 1888, Bernard showed his latest picture in
this style (called Synthetism) to Gauguin, who
realized its possibilities immediately and used it as
the basis for his own* Vision after the Sermon
*(p.56). This remarkable work instantly launched
Gauguin as the leader of a School in which
naturalism gave way to a novel blend of symbolism
and imagination. In the same year, he wrote to a
friend, 'A word of advice: don't paint too much
direct from nature. Art is an abstraction!'*

*Gauguin's prolonged absence from the French
scene meant that his ideas were transmitted
indirectly, through a group of followers called the
Nabis. He met and instructed their leader, Paul*

*Sérusier, during one of his stays in Brittany and,
in turn, Sérusier brought the news of Gauguin's
discoveries to his friends in Paris. The Nabis, who
included such artists as Bonnard and Vuillard, did
not work in a single style, but tended to produce
pictures in which the outside world was reduced to
flattened, decorative forms. Their attitude was
summed up by Maurice Denis, who asserted that 'a
painting, before it is a war horse or a nude . . . is
primarily a flat surface, covered with colours
arranged in a certain order.' This dictum is justly
celebrated since it marked an important step along
the road to abstract art.*

Gauguin's enthusiasm for this semi-abstract

9

pattern-making was evident from many of his Tahitian works (for example, The Day of the God, p.52) and it also played a part in the development of Van Gogh's art. For, despite the tragic results of their tempestuous stay together at Arles, the two painters had much in common.

A Few Sure Strokes

Van Gogh's roots lay firmly in the Dutch Realist tradition. However, after his arrival in Paris in 1886, he absorbed the latest French trends with astonishing speed. By the time he came to leave for Arles, two years later, he had largely abandoned naturalism and was employing the same hard contours and symbolic colours as Gauguin.

The main distinctions between the two painters were in execution and intention. Throughout his career, Van Gogh continued to apply his paint thickly, using it to imbue his images with an expressive power that was entirely lacking in Gauguin's thinly painted canvases. More importantly, Van Gogh's inclinations towards the Romantic led him not to abjure nature, but to seek to extract from it an emotional core. 'I do not invent a picture . . .', he wrote, 'I find it all ready in nature, only it must be disentangled.'

The method which Van Gogh developed for this 'disentangling' process was modelled on the clarity of Japanese prints. 'Their work is as simple as breathing', he noted, 'and they do a figure in a few sure strokes. . .' It was the desire to emulate these 'few sure strokes' that inspired the turbulent, sweeping rhythms which invaded Van Gogh's last, tragic works (pp.93-7). Here, the artist was investing nature with the same furious energy that tormented his own brain, and this correlation of the emotions with the physical world was later to inspire Munch and the Expressionists.

Cézanne, too, transformed nature to suit his needs, but he found Van Gogh's art too neurotic and his own aims were closer to those of Seurat. Both men passed through an Impressionist phase before rejecting the movement as too spontaneous and capricious, and both men were great respecters of tradition. Cézanne's declared aim was to 'make something solid out of Impressionism, and permanent, like museum art'.

Art as Geometry

In pursuing this end, Cézanne retained some typically Impressionist features in his working methods. For example, he never abandoned the practice of plein-air painting and, after his youthful Romantic period, he never introduced imaginary elements into his pictures. Like the Impressionists, he returned to the same subjects again and again. However, where Monet's sequences of paintings were designed to illustrate the widest possible range of lighting and atmospheric effects, Cézanne's aim was quite the reverse. For, by concentrating his energies on a few, oft-repeated themes, he meant to strip away the infinite shifts of light and weather conditions, and arrive at the essential structures that exist within nature.

Increasingly, Cézanne saw these basic forms in geometric terms – as cylinders, spheres and cones – and used them as components in all his compositions. Accordingly, he treated a portrait as just another kind of still-life, while the torsos of his bathers (p.32) held precisely the same formal interest for him as the trunks of the nearby trees. By breaking his subjects down into simple, planar shapes, in this way, Cézanne was creating a new pictorial language that would prove invaluable to Braque, Picasso and the Cubists.

The Post-Impressionists were, therefore, a diverse group, sharing little more than a dissatisfaction with naturalism. However, their fruitful lines of enquiry prompted painters of the next generation to explore different avenues and lay at the root of most modern movements in art.

A favourite subject
(below) Cézanne painted Mont Sainte-Victoire near his home over 60 times. This version dates from 1885-7.

Courtauld Institute Galleries

Scala

Cézanne: Self-portrait at 40/Bern Kunst Museum

P. Cézanne

1839-1906

The illegitimate son of a wealthy, domineering father, Paul Cézanne studied law and worked in the family bank in Aix-en-Provence before moving north to paint in Paris. His wildly erotic early works – and his tense, neurotically suspicious character – earned him a reputation as an eccentric. But he struggled for years to master his medium, and at last emerged as one of the greatest artists of the 19th century.

Through contact with the Impressionists, he began to paint nature and gradually developed a completely new pictorial language, which was to establish him as the 'father of modern art'. He spent most of his mature years working alone in remote Provence, and dedicated his life to art. Fame came late: in 1895 a one-man show revealed his genius to an unsuspecting public. He died at 67, after being caught in a storm while painting.

The Angry Provincial

Throughout his childhood, Cézanne lived in fear of his powerful, overbearing father. He grew up an angry, intense and unsociable man, whose only real attachment was to his art.

Paul Cézanne was born on 19 January 1839 at Aix-en-Provence, a small town a few miles inland from Marseilles, in the South of France. His father, Louis-Auguste Cézanne, was a prosperous hat retailer on his way up in the world, who in 1848 became the proprietor of Aix's only bank. Paul's mother, Anne-Elisabeth-Honorine Aubert, had been Louis-Auguste's mistress until their marriage in 1844, when Paul was five. And in a stuffy little provincial town like Aix, Paul was probably made aware that he was the barely legitimate son of an upstart family – one reason, perhaps, for his notorious touchiness.

FRIENDS FROM CHILDHOOD

At the age of 13, Cézanne became a boarder at Bourbon College in Aix. He proved an excellent scholar and, though not very sociable, formed some close friendships that were to last for most of his life. The most important was with Emile Zola, who later became a famous novelist. In their free time, Cézanne, Zola and a third friend, Baptistin Baille, rambled, swam and fished by the little River Arc, declaiming poetry and dreaming of future greatness. These remained Cézanne's happiest memories, and the many bathing scenes in his later paintings are touched with nostalgia.

At first, Cézanne and his friends believed he was destined to be a poet. Gradually, however, his interest shifted to art and he began to attend free

Bernard Rouget

classes at the local drawing academy. Letters from Zola, who had gone to Paris to study and work, filled him with dreams of leaving Aix for a painter's life in a fourth-floor studio. But Cézanne could not break away from his family. He lived in fear of his domineering father, who had no interest in art and respected nothing but money.

Louis-Auguste's own financial success was symbolized by the Jas de Bouffan, a grand house and estate outside Aix, which became the family home in 1859. Cézanne spent that year as a law student, and passed his first examinations before confessing to his parents that his artistic ambitions were serious. The declaration caused a long family wrangle, but in April 1861 he was finally permitted to go to Paris and given a small allowance. His

Bernard Rouget

Living in style
Cézanne's family home was a huge 18th-century manor, lying just outside Aix – the Jas de Bouffan. The house remained in the family's possession until 1899.

Mont Sainte-Victoire
(below) The little town of Aix, where Cézanne was born, was dominated by the nearby Mont Sainte-Victoire. Cézanne was fascinated by its noble architectural form and painted it from every conceivable viewpoint.

Domestic scene
(right) This detail from Cézanne's gentle painting of a Girl at the Piano *(1869-71), may show his younger sister Marie, in the comfortable drawing-room of the Jas de Bouffan. Cézanne was very dependent on Marie.*

father and mother escorted him to the big city and settled him in.

Six months later Cézanne was back in Aix. Despite Zola's encouragement, he had failed to make much contact with fellow-artists in Paris, or to overcome the fits of black depression in which he ripped up his canvases. Full of self-doubt, he had fled back home. But a tedious year spent working in his father's bank convinced him to try again and in November 1862 – at the age of 23 – he embarked in earnest on his career as a painter.

On his return to Paris, Cézanne failed the entrance examination to the official painting school, the Ecole des Beaux-Arts. He never made the attempt again, but was much more persistent in submitting paintings to the Salon. The annual exhibition was the main opportunity for artists to become known to the general public. But year after year, the Salon jury refused to show Cézanne's paintings and it was typical that, while he was desperate for recognition, he invited the rejection

he feared. He loudly proclaimed the stupidity of the official system, gave his paintings provocative titles, delivered them at the last minute and wrote rude letters to the Superintendent of Fine Arts.

There were other contradictory elements in Cézanne's character, which made him a trial to his fellow-artists. He was timid yet cantankerous, with a dislike of interference which eventually became a pathological loathing of being touched. He harboured terrible doubts about the value of his work, yet he could say 'There is only one painter in the world: myself', and suspect other artists of plotting to steal his ideas. In company he could be deliberately awkward, posing as a shabby provincial boor and thickening his nasal Aixois accent. On one occasion he refused to shake hands with the elegant Manet, on the grounds that he, Cézanne, had not washed for eight days.

In the 1860s, Manet was the arch-rebel of French painting, admired by younger artists such as Monet and Renoir, so Cézanne's rudeness may

Father and son
(above left) Cézanne's father was a wealthy self-made man, who worked his way up from running a hat-making business to owning a bank. Cézanne was terrified of him. As a young man (above), Paul's face had a frightened, nervous expression.

well have been caused by jealousy. Manet, Degas and their friends met regularly in the evenings at the Café Guerbois, and Cézanne was first brought there by Camille Pissarro. At the café, Cézanne behaved as strangely as ever, listening to the discussions in silence until he heard some remark that outraged him, when he would grab his hat and rush away. 'They're a lot of bastards; they dress as smartly as solicitors', he once said of the Guerbois group.

Even in his twenties, Cézanne was known – by the few who knew him at all – as a hopeless eccentric. The good-natured Renoir later declared, 'From the very start, even before I had seen his painting, I felt he was a genius,' but even he commented on Cézanne's oddity. His movements seemed restricted, said Renoir, as though he were encased by an invisible shell. All descriptions of Cézanne suggest that he was subject to tremendous inner pressures, which he struggled to control. His paintings of the 1860s mirror this inner turmoil: corpses, murders, rapes and orgies executed with a fearful clumsy power, were like nothing else being done by his contemporaries.

Then, at the age of 30, Cézanne radically changed both his habits and his painting style. In 1869 he met a young model and seamstress named Hortense Fiquet, who became his mistress. The relationship proved to be long-lasting, even though the couple seem to have been complete opposites: while he was withdrawn and suspicious, she was gregarious and – according to Cézanne – interested in 'nothing but Switzerland and lemonade'. This was his first and only serious affair, for he was always ill at ease with women and afraid that they would 'get their hooks into him'.

Cézanne now gradually abandoned the morbid

Cézanne and Zola

Emile Zola (1840-1902), the famous novelist, was a boyhood friend of Cézanne. Both their families lived in Aix, and the two boys went to the same secondary school. Temperamentally quite different, they were drawn together, Zola wrote, 'by secret affinities'. Their friendship lasted until 1886, when Zola's novel *L'Oeuvre* was published. Its hero, a failed artist who was driven to suicide, was clearly modelled on Cézanne. The painter was deeply hurt and ended their relationship.

Friends from school-days
Cézanne formed some of his most enduring friendships as a boarder at the Bourbon College in Aix. This painting of Paul Alexis Reading to Emile Zola *(c.1869) shows two of his old friends, now successful men in their thirties.*

Zola's shocking novels
(below) Zola's novels were famous for their down-to-earth naturalism – but this 'sordid reality' often shocked the critics. His huge output included the 20 novels in the Rougon-Macquart *series, among them* La Terre *(1888).*

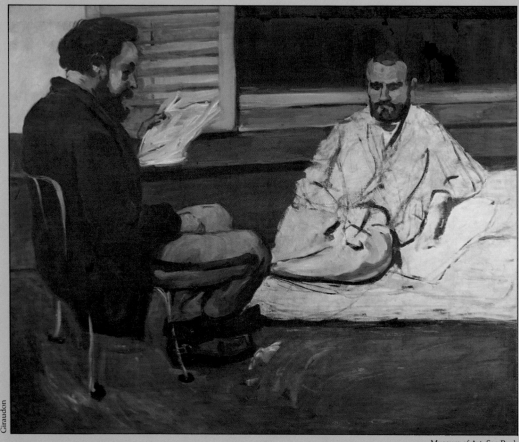

Giraudon

Jean-Loup Charmet

Museum of Art, Sao Paulo

Bernard Rouget

An unconventional marriage
(below) When he was 30, Cézanne took the 19-year-old Hortense Fiquet as his mistress. Three years later she gave birth to their illegitimate son Paul, but Cézanne kept his new family secret. He married Hortense in 1886 – after 17 years together.

Cézanne/Portrait of Mme. Cézanne/Henry P. McIlhenny Collection, Philadelphia

A move to Gardanne
(above) After his marriage to Hortense, Cézanne moved from the Jas de Bouffan to the picturesque hill-town of Gardanne. He lived there for over a year and painted some of his most ordered and geometric landscapes.

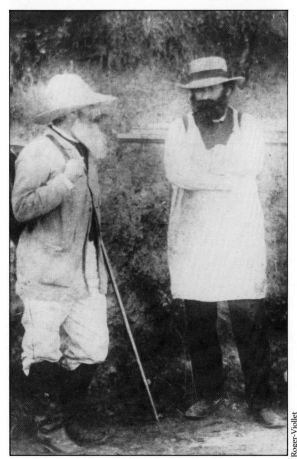

Working with Pissarro
(right) In 1872, shortly after the birth of his son, Cézanne moved with his family to Pontoise, where the artist Camille Pissarro lived. Over the next couple of years, the two men worked side by side, painting in the open air. Pissarro, who was nine years older than Cézanne, is seen here on the left, with a white beard.

Roger-Viollet

sexual fantasies of his early work and turned increasingly to landscape subjects, painting in the open air like the Impressionists. Many of his earliest landscapes were done at L'Estaque, a fishing village near Marseilles, where he spent much of 1870. The visit was not entirely voluntary, for the village served Cézanne as a refuge, where he could avoid conscription during France's war against Prussia.

AN ILLEGITIMATE SON

In 1872 Hortense bore Cézanne a son, also named Paul, whom the artist always adored. But he remained so terrified of his own father that he did not dare to tell the old man that he had a family. Consequently he had to support Hortense and Paul from his none-too-generous allowance as a bachelor. Amazingly, this situation remained unchanged for years, and when Cézanne was in Aix, he would lodge Hortense elsewhere.

The year Paul was born, Cézanne took his new family to Pontoise, a village in the countryside near Paris, where Camille Pissarro lived. Over the next two years the two men worked side by side for long periods; Cézanne stayed first at Pontoise and later at nearby Auvers. This was a unique episode in his life, for Pissarro, a benevolent father figure, was the only master Cézanne ever accepted. He introduced Cézanne to the techniques of Impressionist painting, and ensured that his

15

protégé's works were shown at the first Impressionist exhibition in 1874.

Cézanne's experiences with Pissarro were decisive in his artistic development. Though he was to move beyond Impressionism, he remained devoted to the practice of painting directly from nature. On most fine days he would set out with his pack on his back, or loaded on a donkey, often painting the same subject again and again. His personality remained as difficult as ever, but as an artist Cézanne found a new strength and discipline in contact with nature, and displayed a stronger sense of order in his paintings.

FAILURE AT THE SALON

During the next 10 years or so, Cézanne led a solitary, unsettled existence, dividing his time between Paris, Aix and their environs. Quietly and carefully, he developed his own unique way of painting 'constructions after nature'. But publicly he remained a failure. After years of trying, he had only one work accepted for the Salon – and that was through someone pulling strings for him.

The year 1886 brought three critical events in Cézanne's life. First, Emile Zola published a novel that ended their long friendship. Now a successful man of letters, Zola had not forgotten his childhood companion, offering him both friendship and hospitality at his château at Médan outside Paris. But in his novel *L'Oeuvre*, Zola's main character was a failed artist, who bore all too many resemblances to Cézanne. The painter wrote to thank Zola for sending him a copy, but he was deeply offended, and never saw Zola again.

The second event took place a few weeks later, when Cézanne, who had at last admitted the existence of his illicit family, married Hortense. It is not clear why he chose to do so, for the relationship had long since lost its fervour, and in 1885 Cézanne seems to have made a half-hearted attempt at an affair with one of the servants at the

A studio museum
Cézanne had his last studio specially built for him on a road outside Aix, which commanded magnificent views, both of the town and his beloved Mont Sainte-Victoire. The Chemin des Lauves on which it was built has been renamed Avenue Paul Cézanne, and the studio itself has been preserved as a museum.

The Black Château
(below) After selling the Jas de Bouffan, Cézanne tried to buy this grand old house – the Château Noir – which stands in the pine forests between Aix and the Mont Sainte-Victoire. He had already rented a room there, which he used as a base during his painting trips. When attempts to buy the château failed, the artist bought land on the Chemin des Lauves instead.

Bernard Rouget

Jas de Bouffan. Finally, in October 1886, Louis-Auguste Cézanne died, leaving his son wealthy and independent at last. 'My father was a genius,' Cézanne remarked sardonically. 'He left me an income of 25,000 francs!'

THE LIFE OF A RECLUSE

The events of 1886 encouraged Cézanne to withdraw more completely into his shell. Hortense and Paul lived in Paris most of the time, while the painter stayed with his family at the Jas de Bouffan; his sister Marie looked after him, and seems to have replaced his father as a dominating influence. Cézanne visited Paris less and less often, and even stopped sending pictures to the Salon. He now mixed mainly with his old cronies from Aix. In 1890 he made his only trip abroad – to Switzerland, with Hortense – but generally he succeeded in cutting himself off from the outside world.

Within a few years Cézanne was half-forgotten, and some of the younger artists who became interested in his work were under the impression that he was dead. He was in his late fifties before his paintings began to attract a little of the attention they deserved. Then the famous art dealer Ambroise Vollard took him up, and in 1895 organized a one-man show in Paris. It was the first time Cézanne's paintings had been seen in the capital for nearly 20 years, and though his works were not necessarily understood, people seemed to sense their greatness. In 1897, Vollard visited Cézanne at his studio in Fontainebleau, and bought every painting there.

From time to time, young admirers made a pilgrimage to see the legendary master at Aix, and

Bernard Rouget

Fame at Last

Until the 1890s, Cézanne's work was seen only by a handful of people. Although his paintings could be bought in Père Tanguy's tiny Paris art shop, he was virtually unknown in the capital – indeed, people spoke of him as if he were already dead.

In 1895, the art dealer Ambroise Vollard – on the insistence of Cézanne's loyal supporter Pissarro – organized a one-man show for him in Paris. Cézanne sent 150 canvases from Aix, and although Vollard's shop was too small to show them all, the exhibition marked the beginning of his increasing fame.

Bridgeman Art Library

Petit Palais, Paris

A lonely end
Cézanne caught a fatal chill after being drenched in a storm while working on a landscape. His sister Marie summoned his wife and son from Paris, but Cézanne died before they arrived, on 22 October 1906. A sad bouquet of plastic flowers marks his tombstone.

Sale of the century
(above) On 15 October 1958, 1,400 art lovers and thousands of television viewers witnessed a record-breaking sale at Sotheby's auction rooms in London. The American collector Paul Mellon bought Cézanne's Boy in a Red Waistcoat for $616,000 – then the highest price ever paid for a modern painting.

Portrait of Ambroise Vollard (1899)
The art dealer endured over 100 sittings for this portrait, after which Cézanne declared – with characteristic perfectionism – that he was not displeased with the shirt front.

Cézanne seems to have enjoyed their homage. But in other respects his old age was uneventful. In 1899 he was forced to sell the Jas de Bouffan to settle his mother's estate. He rented a flat in Aix with a studio attached, and in 1901 bought a plot of land on the hill-side of the Chemin des Lauves outside Aix. He had another studio built on the site, and walked there to work each day.

A FATAL CHILL

In later years, as his health deteriorated, Cézanne travelled by carriage instead of walking. But one day, angered by a small fare increase, he rashly gave up the carriage. As a result, he was caught in the open during a long downpour and was drenched so badly that he collapsed and was brought home in a laundry cart. His attempt to work again the following day made matters worse, and he died of pneumonia a week later, on 22 October 1906. His wife and son were in Paris.

Bernard Rouget

The Geometry of Nature

**Toiling alone on the hillsides of Provence, Cézanne developed a
new way of painting the natural world. He sought beneath the
surface for the essential elements of nature's geometry.**

'In all the history of art, there has seldom been a painter whose early style differed so greatly from that of his maturity', wrote the critic René Huyghe. Indeed, it is hard to see any resemblance between the subtle, deliberately balanced canvases of Cézanne's mature years, and the morbidly violent and erotic pictures of his twenties, which often give the impression of having been created in a frenzy. For a time Cézanne abandoned the brush for a palette knife, slapping on the paint. And as if to emphasize his personal involvement with these fantasies, he often included a picture of himself within the painting: he appears as the balding onlooker in *A Modern Olympia* (below).

Gradually, Cézanne turned to the outside world for inspiration. As early as October 1866, he wrote to his friend Emile Zola that 'pictures painted inside, in the studio, will never be as good as those done outside'. But, oddly enough, it was not until the 1870s that he followed up this insight. By that time, Pissarro and his friends Monet and Renoir had discovered most of the techniques of Impressionism, which Cézanne was to learn during his association with Pissarro at Pontoise.

Impressionism turned Cézanne into an outdoor painter – a dusty, weather-beaten figure with a broad-brimmed hat and heavy boots who tramped the countryside every day with his pack slung across his shoulders. But though Cézanne never abandoned this way of working, he soon became dissatisfied with some aspects of Impressionism. He had a stronger sense of construction than his contemporaries, whose paintings tended to dissolve objects in a play of dazzling light. He wanted to retain the brightness and freshness of Impressionism but make of it 'something solid and durable, like the art of the museum'.

BEYOND IMPRESSIONISM

He adapted the distinct, blocked, dash-like strokes, which broke up forms in Impressionist paintings, using them instead to construct form. In the late 1870s, they became a repeated pattern of regular oblongs of paint, arranged in parallel across his pictures, as in the *Château at Médan* (p.21). As well as giving solidity to the forms in the picture, the repetition and regularity of these paint marks emphasized the painting's surface unity.

Indeed, as his personal style developed, Cézanne became determined that the flat, two-dimensional nature of the painting should not be

Painting in the open
*Cézanne first began
painting out of doors in
the 1870s, encouraged by
Pissarro. From then on,
he set out almost daily.*

A Modern Olympia (1872-73)
(below) This parody of Manet's Olympia *provoked
a storm of abuse at the 1874 Impressionist exhibition:
critics described Cézanne as a drug-crazed lunatic.*

**Mont Sainte-Victoire
(1885-87)**
*(right) This rugged
mountain near his family
home held strong
emotional associations for
Cézanne. He described it
to Zola in 1878 as a
'stunning motif' and
painted it obsessively for
the next three decades. In
this version, the contours
of the distant mountain
are echoed by the branches
of the pine tree.*

Réunion des Musées Nationaux

Musée d'Orsay, Paris

denied. He was not interested in imitating the real world: he called his paintings 'constructions after nature', in which essential elements from the three-dimensional world were reassembled on a flat canvas. And to represent the real spatial relationships between objects without breaking up the flatness of the canvas, he devised his own method: the so-called 'flat-depth', which has been called 'one of the miracles of art'.

Cézanne achieved his aim in various ways: by overlapping patches of paint so that one appears to be in front of the other, by depicting objects from several angles at once, apparently pulling them towards the surface, and by exploiting the visual phenomenon whereby *warm* colours (reds and yellows) appear to come towards us, while *cold* colours (blues and greens) seem to recede. And instead of modelling his subjects with light and shade, Cézanne 'modulated' form with colour.

This unique system of painting did not come to Cézanne in a flash of inspiration: he developed it slowly and laboriously – the same way, in fact, that he painted each picture. He would work on a painting for months, sometimes years, always addressing the entire canvas simultaneously, not painting it section by section. A dab of colour here

Lefevre Gallery (Private Collection)

Courtauld Institute, London

Harlequin (1888-90)
Cézanne's son Paul modelled for this painting, but his features have been simplified beyond recognition into a haunting image of the lonely clown.

Courtauld Institute, London

Patches of paint
(above) In late works such as The Turn in the Road *(1900-6) Cézanne developed a freer system of painting, using a sequence of squarish paint marks, often set against bare patches of canvas.*

Still-life with Onions
(left) Cézanne painted almost 200 still-lifes. Making repeated use of a small set of household objects, along with everyday fruit and vegetables, he created an infinitely varied series of compositions.

Réunion des Musées Nationaux

Musée d'Orsay, Paris

19

would be balanced by another colour there, and so on, building up the painting as a coherent whole. This painstaking process was at the opposite extreme to his early emotional outpourings.

A NEW FREEDOM

Yet in Cézanne's later pictures, from the 1880s onwards, a new kind of expressive freedom emerged. Where his first paintings had been overstated and clumsily executed, these late paintings show the economy and subtlety that comes only when an artist has mastered his medium. His paint became thinner, his colours richer, and the rigidly regular strokes of paint became more loosely painted patches of colour – often set beside patches of bare canvas, as in *The Turn in the Road* (p.19). It was a revolutionary way of painting, which laid the foundations for the major art movements of the 20th century, from Cubism to abstract art.

Perhaps because of his strong desire to organize nature, Cézanne became one of the great masters of a type of painting that had largely fallen into

Réunion des Musées Nationaux

Musée d'Orsay, Paris

Woman with a Coffee Pot (1890-94)
Cézanne treats this portrait in the same way as a still-life. The woman – his housekeeper – is as angular and impersonal as the cup beside her, with its unnaturally upright spoon. He once wrote that 'Painting stands for no other end than itself. The artist paints an apple or a head: it is simply a pretext for line and colour, nothing more'.

COMPARISONS

The Fashion for Still-Life

Still-life painting has had a chequered career in the history of art. After achieving great popularity in Holland during the 17th century, its reputation had declined by the 19th: Cézanne was largely responsible for rescuing it from second-class status.

However, unlike the Dutch artists such as de Heem, who had stunned the public with their virtuoso rendition of life-like surface textures, Cézanne made no attempt to create an illusion that his food and crockery actually existed on the canvas. Instead, he concentrated on colour and composition – his simple objects with their stark geometry inspired Picasso's early Cubist still-lifes.

Giraudon-Paris/Öffentliche Kunstsammlung, Basel/©DACS 1988

Wallace Collection, London

Jan Davidsz de Heem (1606-1683/4) Still-life with a Lobster
This exotic still-life achieves its appeal from its range of immaculately painted surface textures – from the moist softness of the fruit to the hard, shiny shell of the lobster.

Pablo Picasso (1881-1973) Bread and Compotier with Fruit on a Table (1908)
Instead of imitating surface appearances, Picasso analyzed structures. He developed the principles of Cubist still-life from Cézanne's paintings.

Burrell Collection, Glasgow

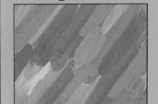

Parallel, oblong brush-strokes characterize Cézanne's first mature painting style.

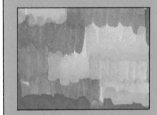

Later, he began to use more loosely defined, and often squarish patches of colour.

neglect – the still-life. He could choose and arrange natural elements himself, not hesitating to wedge them or prop them up to secure exactly the arrangement he wanted.

Human beings were irritatingly more difficult to arrange. 'Apples don't move!' Cézanne once snapped at a weary sitter. Impatient and uneasy with people, until late in life he could only tolerate his own family or close friends as portrait models.

Cézanne was even less able to cope with nude models, and his bathing scenes were painted with the aid of photographs. These scenes represent a more openly emotional strain in his work, probably related to the painted orgies and violence of his youth. But as an artist, at least, Cézanne had tamed his demons, and in a picture such as *The Great Bathers* (p.32) the figures have become part of the landscape, sharing its beauty and order.

Particular places were important to Cézanne. He painted almost exclusively in the environs of Paris and in his native South. The hard outlines of the Provençal landscape encouraged his quest for a 'solid and durable' art: 'I am passionately fond of the contours of this country,' he wrote. He painted certain places many times – above all Mont Sainte-Victoire, the mountain that dominates some 60 of Cézanne's paintings.

Even at the end of his life, Cézanne was still advancing – yet he still grumbled. 'I am beginning to glimpse the Promised Land,' he wrote 'but why so late and with such difficulty?'

Château at Médan
(above and right) Cézanne painted Zola's summer residence on the River Seine in about 1880. His methodical repetition of parallel, oblong brushstrokes gives the painting a distinctly woven appearance. And this effect is strengthened by the grid of vertical and horizontal lines – in the poplar trees, houses and river bank – which binds the composition together.

THE MAKING OF A MASTERPIECE

Apples and Oranges

The rich design of *Apples and Oranges* (see pp.30-31) is built up from the simple shapes of everyday objects which Cézanne kept with him, and painted time and again in the quiet of his own studio.

He does not hide the fact that the painting is deliberately contrived and 'unnatural': the objects appear to be slipping off the table, which itself is seen from a very strange angle. Shapes appear distorted as they are shown from more than one viewpoint simultaneously – for example, the base of the fruit dish is seen from the side, while its bowl is viewed from above.

The use of distortion and shifting viewpoint was carefully thought out. It allowed Cézanne to depict natural forms and the relationships between them, while stressing the essential difference between reality and a painting – an arrangement of colour on a canvas.

Lauros-Giraudon

Musée d'Orsay, Paris

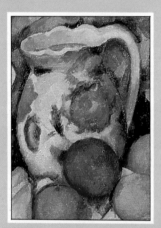

Painted flowers
Cézanne incorporated this jug in many of his still-lifes, setting its painted flowers against 'real' fruit in a kind of visual pun.

Creating shapes with colour
Colour – not light and shade – defines the geometric forms of the fruit. The apple on the lower right, for example, is described by overlapping colours ranging from deep red at the edges, through orange tones, to a yellow highlight.

Art Institute of Chicago/Helen Birch Bartlett Memorial Collection

Artificial arrangements
Cézanne's method of setting up his still-lifes is made particularly obvious in Still-life with Basket of Apples (1890-94). The basket is propped up by a block, while the plate of biscuits rests on a book.

A revealing description of Cézanne at work comes from the painter Louis le Bail: 'The cloth was lightly draped on the table, then Cézanne arranged the fruit, contrasting tones, setting greens against reds. He turned, tipped and balanced the pieces of fruit as he wanted – using coins of one or two sous to help.'

Multicoloured whites
The almost sculpted folds of white cloth are created by a subtle play of warm and cool colours. Pinks and pale yellows suggest the outward curves, while blues and greens describe deep hollows in the drapery.

Cézanne's favourite props
The floral jug appears again in this late watercolour (1902-6). More freely painted than the earlier picture, its thin washes and broken contours are firmly held by the pure, rounded volumes and straight lines.

Carafe, Cruche et Citron/Thyssen-Bornemisza Collection/Lugano, Switzerland

'See in nature the cylinder, the sphere and the cone.'

Paul Cézanne

A geometric framework
(below) The complexity of this still-life is carefully controlled by its underlying geometry. Some of the major geometric shapes have been superimposed: they give stability to the precarious arrangement.

The artist's studio
(right) Even when Cézanne moved between Paris and Aix, he took many of his props with him. They have been preserved in his last studio in the Chemin des Lauves (now Avenue Paul Cézanne in Aix).

Art work by Trevor Lawrence

Giraudon

Gallery

Cézanne's distinctive style, which imposed a new kind of order on nature, establishes him as one of the founders of modern art. His painting reached maturity in the 1870s: the portrait of Madame Cézanne shows him simplifying and distorting her image in the interests of artistic unity. Boy in a Red Waistcoat continues the same trend.

Madame Cézanne in a Red Armchair *1877*
28½″ × 22″ Museum of Fine Arts, Boston

Painted nine years before they married, Cézanne's portrait of Hortense is remarkably impersonal. He was less concerned with revealing his mistress's character than with the way the cool tones and flattened stripes of the dress are enveloped by the warm pinks and rounded shapes of the armchair.

Cézanne was happiest painting people and places he knew well: the sturdy Provençal Card Players, for example, and The Great Pine. He was less productive away from his home ground, although paintings such as the Lake at Annecy bear his unmistakable stamp. And he produced numerous works in his studio, where he was free to organize the natural elements for still-lifes such as Apples and Oranges.

Around the turn of the century, Cézanne's painting became freer, more fluid and even more simplified. This can be seen in The Great Bathers and Mont Sainte-Victoire, where his system of painting with patches of pure colour paves the way for abstract art.

Boy in a Red Waistcoat *1890-1895*
36¼″ × 28¾″ Collection of Mr and Mrs Paul Mellon,
Upperville, Virginia

Although he rarely used professional sitters, Cézanne made four oil portraits of this young Italian model, Michelangelo di Rosa. The boy stands with hand on hip, in the classic pose of the life-class nude, the curve of his body counterbalanced by the swinging drapery.

The Card Players *1890-1892*
22¾″ × 27″ Courtauld Institute
Galleries, London

Cézanne's paintings of local Provençal men quietly concentrating on a game of cards are among his most popular works. He has stripped the scene to its bare essentials – two men facing each other across a table. Yet, quiet and provincial as it first appears, this is a revolutionary painting. For the sake of artistic unity, Cézanne has abandoned traditional perspective – for example, the table appears irregularly shaped as it is seen from several angles at once. Its top is tilted forwards, while the men's bent knees appear flattened – one above the other – against the front of the picture. And although the painting seems to be made up of greys and browns, rough patches of blue, red and green, as well as areas of bare canvas, give the picture a subtle vitality.

The Great Pine *1892-96*
33″ × 36¼″ Museum of Art, Sao Paulo, Brazil

*This romantic image of a great tree buffeted by the forces of nature,
yet rising above them, originates from a poem which Cézanne wrote
in his youth about 'The tree shaken by the fury of the winds'. The
apparently simple composition, centring on the tree's buckled trunk,
evokes a powerful sense of tension.*

Lake at Annecy *1896*
25¼″ × 32″ Courtauld Institute Galleries, London

*Cézanne painted this alpine lake near the Swiss frontier to 'divert'
himself during one of the rare trips he made during his last years.
Although he found the mountainous scenery claustrophobic, he
created a memorable image, particularly striking because of the
apparent solidity of the water.*

Apples and Oranges *1895-1900*
28¾″ × 36¼″ Musée d'Orsay, Paris

This is one of the most sumptuous of all Cézanne's still-lifes. The complex arrangement of fruit, dishes, jug and drapery on a table which slopes dramatically upwards from the left is given stability by the bold zigzag line created by the edges of the white cloth. It was painted in Aix: some of the objects in the painting are still preserved there, in his Chemin des Lauves studio.

The Great Bathers *1898-1905*
82″ × 98″ Philadelphia Museum of Art

*Nearly seven feet high and over eight feet long, this is the largest of a
late series of paintings in which Cézanne attempted to integrate nude
figures with landscape. He achieved his aim: figures and landscape
almost merge as the arch of the trees soars up from the simplified
curves of the women's bodies.*

Mont Sainte-Victoire *1904-06*
28⅞″ × 35¾″ Philadelphia Museum of Art

Cézanne was obsessed with this huge limestone mountain, which stands some 10 miles from Aix, and painted it over 60 times with increasing freedom. In this late work, the sequence of fluid paint patches, which are used to suggest the natural elements of the landscape, become an almost abstract mosaic of colour.

The Landscape of Provence

Unlike the Impressionists, who painted numerous scenes of city life, Cézanne never felt at home in Paris. He returned to his native Provence to find the inspiration which eluded him in the capital.

Paul Cézanne began his painting career at a time when the artistic world was firmly focused on Paris. The early Impressionists all studied there, and even when they travelled into outlying villages, or to the coast of Normandy, they still returned repeatedly to the capital to exhibit – and attempt to sell – their paintings. But Cézanne, shy and socially inept, was never really suited to Parisian life. During the eight years he spent there, from 1863 to 1870, he was happier wandering alone in the hills outside the capital than drinking and debating with the urbane, avant-garde artists of the Café Guerbois.

THE MOUNTAINS AND THE SEA

When the Prussian army invaded France in 1870, Cézanne returned south to his home town of Aix-en-Provence – partly to avoid conscription. The environment he found there was not only more familiar, but offered an atmosphere totally opposite to the metropolitan sophistications of Paris. Instead of the grey chill of the northern winter there was dazzling sunlight and warmth for most of the year; instead of narrow cobbled streets there were massive granite mountains, fast-flowing rivers and the blue Mediterranean Sea; instead of jostling crowds and short-lived fashions there was solitude, a slow pace of life and a reassuring sense of timelessness.

The landscape of Provence became one of the principal inspirations of Cézanne's work. He painted it with a relentless intensity that few artists have devoted to any subject, creating dozens of images of favourite motifs, above all the Mont Sainte-Victoire. In 1886 he wrote to the collector Victor Chocquet, 'there are treasures to be taken away from this country, which has not yet found an interpreter equal to the abundance of riches which it displays', and 30 years later, a few weeks before his death, he was still so entranced with the landscape that he wrote to his son: 'I think I could occupy myself for months without changing my place, simply bending a little more to left or right.'

Yet the hundreds of paintings and drawings Cézanne produced of Provence tell us little about

Jean-Loup Charmet

The Marseillaise
(above) The people of Provence were enthusiastic supporters of the French Revolution. Indeed, the national anthem – a revolutionary marching song – was first used by troops setting out from Marseilles.

Roger Snowdon

A Roman province
Provence derives its name from the days of the Roman Empire, when the region was known as Provincia Romana. Among the many classical remains is this magnificent aqueduct, the Pont du Gard, which was built in about 19BC.

Roger Snowdon

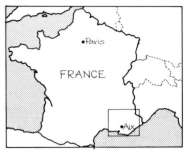

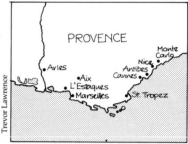

The rugged landscape
The barren countryside of Provence provided continual inspiration to Cézanne, who emphasized the underlying geological forms of the mountains and the coastline in his drawings and paintings.

Ancient relics
(below) These drystone huts, or 'bories', found in the highlands of Provence, testify to the antiquity of human settlement in the region.

the region. He concentrated on the underlying, unchanging structure of the landscape, and did not usually represent a particular time of day or even a particular season. There is nothing anecdotal about his pictures and they usually contain no figures or other evidence of human activity. Houses are often included, but they are treated as part of the landscape, and he never painted the town of Aix itself.

AN INDEPENDENT PEOPLE

Some 500 miles from Paris, isolated from the north by the Alps and the rugged plateau of the Massif Central, Provence was like a separate country in Cézanne's day. Rail links with the north, only recently completed, had done little to break down the attitude of sturdy independence that dated back to Roman times, when the region first earned its name as 'Provincia Romana'. Nor had the lifestyle of its inhabitants changed greatly over the centuries – a description by the Roman historian Posidonius remained as true in the 19th century as the day it was written in the 1st century BC: 'The country is wild and arid. The soil is so stony that you cannot plant anything without striking a rock.' The population had remained largely rural, with peasant agriculture the mainstay of the economy.

Provence's stormy history had, if anything, strengthened its differences from the rest of France. After the Romans, the Goths, Franks and Saracens all left their bloody mark upon the region, attracted by its strategic position between Spain and Italy at the mouth of the River Rhône. Right up until the time of the French Revolution, Provence was troubled by recurring periods of civil disturbances. But the Revolution was welcomed by the southerners, who believed it would lead to more independence from the 'Parigots', as they contemptuously called those from the capital. It was in Marseilles that the French national anthem – the *Marseillaise* – first rang out in 1792. Three years before, the red, white and blue national flag known as the tricolour was raised in the small Provençal town of Martigues.

Even in Cézanne's time, the inhabitants of

Topham Picture Library

Edimage

The Provençal language
In the 19th century, Provençal declined rapidly as a spoken language, but in 1854 the local poet Frédéric Mistral formed a society to revive its use.

Provence maintained a strong sense of regional pride, underpinned by the local dialect, impenetrable to outsiders. Cézanne sometimes used it in the Café Guerbois when he wished to be pointedly anti-social. However, this traditional language was diminishing in use, as the 'standard' Parisian dialect became obligatory for those engaged in commerce. To try to stop the decline, a poet called Frédéric Mistral, with seven other Provençal literary figures, formed a society in 1854 'to raise up, honour and defend the mother

tongue, now so sadly despised and neglected'. The campaign was enthusiastically received and the society's review *L'Armana Prouvencau* (the Provençal Almanac) became fashionable reading, but it could not reverse the steady decline in everyday use of the language.

Although time seemed to have stood still in many parts of Cézanne's Provence, changes were occurring on the coast that were to transform the region's image, as the Riviera became a luxurious holiday playground. The fashion for staying there was started by Lord Brougham, Lord Chancellor of England, who had to stay in Cannes in 1834 during a cholera outbreak which delayed his intended journey into Italy. He liked it so much that he returned regularly for the next 30 years. Monte Carlo became probably the most famous of the resorts associated with conspicuous high-living, and its celebrated casino opened in 1861.

A HAVEN FOR ARTISTS

Although the railway linked Aix with Cannes and Nice, Cézanne was more attracted to the coastline nearer home – especially the village of L'Estaque, of which he painted some memorable pictures. The scenery around L'Estaque was renowned for its beauty, as Zola's description testifies: 'A village just outside of Marseilles, in the centre of an alley of rocks which close the bay . . . The country is superb. The arms of rock stretch out on either side of the gulf, while the islands, extending in width, seem to bar the horizon, and the sea is but a vast basin, a lake of brilliant blue when the weather is fine.'

Although Cézanne was the first painter to make the Provençal landscape a major subject of his work, he was not the only great artist of his period to be attracted to the region. Van Gogh lived at Arles from 1888 to 1890, and was visited there by Gauguin in 1888. Van Gogh had intended forming an artists' colony at Arles, and although

The farming tradition
In Cézanne's time, most of the population still lived in the countryside, eking out a living as peasant farmers. Here a Provençal shepherd leads his flock past the ruins of a Roman watermill in the countryside near Arles.

Roger Snowdon

Antibes has a Picasso museum, for example, and Nice has museums devoted to both Chagall and Matisse. Yet the home town of Provence's greatest artist cannot boast any important examples of his work. Cézanne's studio in Aix (in a street that has been renamed the Avenue Paul Cézanne) is open to the public, but the Musée Granet in Aix has only a few minor paintings and drawings among its predominantly Classical collection of paintings from the 16th to the 19th centuries. The director in Cézanne's day was an arch-conservative who vowed that no Cézanne would ever hang there so long as he had power to prevent it.

Auguste-Henri Pontier kept his word until his death in 1926, by which time Cézanne's master-pieces had been dispersed around the globe. Yet in one way this is not inappropriate, for Cézanne was committed to the enduring and universal values of his landscape rather than its topo-graphical details. His genius belongs to the world, not just one particular place.

Aix-en-Provence
The Cours Mirabeau – a wide avenue with majestic plane trees which runs through the centre of Aix – was a familiar sight for Cézanne. It had been the focal point of the town since the trees were first planted in the 17th century.

this came to nothing, the fact that he and the other two founding figures of modern art worked in Provence has, from the early 20th century, played a part in luring other artists there. Most of the major figures who have worked there have been drawn to the Côte d'Azur in the east of the region. Matisse is particularly associated with Nice, and Picasso with Antibes; Renoir built a villa at Cagnes towards the end of his long life.

Provence today is proud of its artistic heritage.

Monte Carlo
(left) The Casino of Monte Carlo was opened in 1861 for the amusement of the wealthy holidaymakers who were flocking to the south of France. It dominates the tiny state of Monaco, a jewel in the Provençal coastline.

St Tropez
(above) Within a few miles of the quiet beauty spots painted by Cézanne, the Riviera was becoming an increasingly popular holiday destination. Like Cannes and Nice, St Tropez has become a playground for the rich.

A Year in 1900
the Life

As France celebrated her imperial prestige with a huge exhibition in Paris, Europe's colonial powers reaped a bitter harvest abroad. In Peking, Chinese nationalists rose against the foreigners and in South Africa, Britain was locked in a vicious struggle with the Boers. The South African War brought to the dawning century a hideous innovation: the concentration camp.

Mafeking relieved

The defence of Mafeking – besieged by the Boers from 12 October 1899 to 17 May 1900 – became a symbol of Britain's struggle against the Boers. Crowds celebrated in the streets when news reached London that the isolated garrison had finally been relieved.

Edimage

The Mansell Collection

Victories for the Boers

In the first months of the South African War (1899-1902) the Boers – shown here in their distinctive, broad-brimmed hats – inflicted stinging defeats on British forces. They had invaded the Cape Province in a desperate attempt to prevent Britain from annexing the Transvaal.

On 14 April 1900, M. Loubet, the President of the French Republic, opened the greatest international exhibition the world had ever seen. Total attendance at the *Exposition Universelle de Paris*, which ran until 11 November, numbered 50 million – an average daily attendance of 24,000. Visitors toured the site on an electrically-powered moving platform with three tiers, each rolling at a different speed. And for the first time the public saw X-ray photography, wireless telegraphy and cars.

DELIGHTS OF THE EAST

In contrast to these technological achievements there was the exotic exhibition of the colonies, housed near the Eiffel Tower. This included French colonies and protectorates and those of other nations, though the term 'colony' was somewhat loosely defined: alongside the Tunisian pavilion, and those for Madagascar, Algeria, Senegal, the French Congo and India, were pavilions dedicated to Siberia, Egypt, China and Japan.

Life in the colonies was reconstructed with mosques, temples and entire villages, to show how the indigenous population might live. There were Cambodian and Indian dance theatres, a 'diorama' painted with desert scenes flanked by an Arab quarter where visitors could sample the delights of North Africa, and a 'stereorama' composed of a revolving circular backdrop painted to give the impression of travelling by ship along the coast of Algeria.

If colonial adventures were a success in Paris, they were a disaster in London. Since the beginning of the year, the Boer

Mary Evans Picture Library

Paris Universal Exhibition

(above) The Palace of Electricity, with its illuminated fountains, was a centrepiece of the vast 1900 exhibition, which extended over 267 acres along the Champs Elysées and both banks of the River Seine.

Count Zeppelin

(right) Ferdinand von Zeppelin (1838-1917) was a German soldier and airship designer, who fought in three wars – including the American Civil War – before retiring as a lieutenant-general in 1891. In 1900 his famous airship made its maiden flight above Lake Constance, in southern Germany.

Archiv für Kunst und Geschichte

81_Escalier Mobile Electrique.

Jean-Loup Charmet

The first escalator

(above) The electrically-driven moving staircase, patented in the United States during the 1890s, was developed by the Otis Elevator Company and first installed at the Paris Universal Exhibition in 1900.

War in South Africa – a bitter struggle between Dutch and British colonists for control of the Transvaal – had cost thousands of lives. Gold had been discovered there in 1886, transforming the poor agricultural region farmed by the Boers into one of the wealthiest in Africa, and tension had mounted steadily. In October 1899, the High Commissioner Sir Alfred Milner rejected an ultimatum from the Boer leader Paul Kruger to withdraw British troops.

BRITISH UNDER SIEGE

The Boers attacked British positions and in one 'black week' of December 1899 the three divisions of the British Army under Sir Redvers Buller (subsequently known as Sir Reverse Buller)

were defeated and holed up in Ladysmith, Kimberley and Mafeking. Boer forces outnumbered their adversaries by three to one; they were all mounted, familiar with the terrain, and excellent marksmen armed with German Krupps rifles.

In January, Buller failed disastrously to relieve Ladysmith, losing 1,700 men at Spion Kop, and Lord Roberts was sent from England to take overall command. The tide soon turned. Roberts reformed the army and outmanoeuvred General Cronje, the Boer military leader, before relieving Kimberley on 15 February; 12 days later Cronje was forced to surrender. On 28 February, Buller's fifth attempt to relieve Ladysmith succeeded, and from March until June Roberts continued his advance through Bloemfontein, Johannesburg and Pretoria.

On 17 May, Mafeking was relieved, ending a 215 day siege

Jean-Loup Charmet

The Commonwealth of Australia
(below) In 1900, a British Imperial Act declared that the colonies of Western Australia, South Australia, Victoria, New South Wales and Queensland should be federated into the Commonwealth of Australia, but the new parliament did not meet until 1908. The legislation was so complex that the Australian citizen could be forgiven for concluding – with The Puzzled Kangaroo in this Punch *cartoon – 'I suppose it's what I wanted; but I'm hanged if I know what I've got!'*

Ann Ronan Picture Library

JUNE 27, 1900.] PUNCH, OR THE LONDON CHARIVARI. 453

THE PUZZLED KANGAROO.
"WELL, I SUPPOSE IT'S WHAT I WANTED; BUT I'M HANGED IF I KNOW WHAT I'VE GOT!"

Puccini's *Tosca*
(above and right) Giacomo Puccini (1858-1924) was the last of the great Italian opera composers. Tosca, one of his most famous works, was first performed in 1900 at the Teatro Costanzi in Rome; it tells the story of a beautiful, but jealous, singer who is tormented by a cruel police chief. The sensational story of love, lust and betrayal echoed the tensions in the composer's own life, for Puccini was renowned for his passionate pursuit of blood sports, fast cars and women.

Archiv für Kunst und Geschichte

for Robert Baden-Powell (founder of the Boy Scout movement) and his soldiers. The *Daily Express*, Britain's jingoistic newspaper founded the previous month, blazoned the news 'History's most heroic defence ends in triumph', and when the news was announced from the stage in London's theatres, wildly enthusiastic crowds rushed out to celebrate in the street.

By September the last of the Boer army in the field had been defeated, all British prisoners of war had been released, Kruger had fled to Portuguese territory, and the Transvaal had finally been annexed to Britain. Roberts handed over command to General Kitchener for what was assumed to be a simple mopping-up operation. But the war was far from over. In fact, the period from September 1900 until May 1902 proved the most bitter of all, for the British were now faced with fierce resistance from the Boer guerilla fighters. Kitchener fought back with a drastic scorched earth policy, even introducing his notorious 'concentration camps', where rebels including women and children were coralled in such atrocious conditions that over 20,000 died.

REBELLION IN CHINA

In the autumn, Kruger travelled to Europe to seek help for the Boers. The continent was generally pro-Boer but even his most likely supporter, Kaiser Wilhelm II of Germany, refused to see him. Events far away in China had signalled an urgent need for European co-operation, with the first stirrings of the 'Boxer' rebellion – its name deriving from 'the fist of righteous

Archiv für Kunst und Geschichte

The Boxer rebellion
(left) A revolt by Chinese 'Boxer' nationalists, pledged to 'protect the country, destroy the foreigner', broke out in Peking during June 1900, when the German consul was murdered. An international force quickly crushed the uprising; here European troops oversee the execution of the captured Chinese assassin.

Freud on dreams
Sigmund Freud (1856-1939), the Austrian founder of psychoanalysis, published his classic work The Interpretation of Dreams *in 1900, while working as a private doctor. Two years later he was appointed professor of neuropathology at the University of Vienna, where he remained until the Nazi annexation of Austria in 1938. He died in London the following year.*

Archiv für Kunst und Geschichte

harmony'. The rebels were pledged to rid China of foreigners.

On 20 June the Boxers had murdered the German consul in Peking, as a prelude to a siege of foreign legations. In their xenophobic zeal, they also destroyed much of their own heritage – an arson attack on a foreign warehouse inadvertently burnt the business quarter of Tientsin to the ground, and also destroyed the Chinese equivalent of the national museum.

END OF THE MANCHUS

The revolt was short-lived, for in August an international force, which included American, Japanese and European troops, seized Peking and hanged the rebels' heads in cages from its walls. The rising signalled the end of the Manchu dynasty.

The London 'Tube'

The Central London underground railway – running through tunnels constructed from metal tubes – was opened in 1900, and the line was electrified the same year. London's first sections of tunnel had been built of bricks and the trains were drawn by coal-fired locomotives, which belched out smoke and steam.

For Europe's royalty too, 1900 was an ominous year. Queen Victoria was reaching the end of her long reign – she died the following year, aged 82. On 4 April there was an assassination attempt on the Prince of Wales; on 29 July King Humbert I of Italy was shot dead by an anarchist named Bresci; and on 16 November a woman threw a hatchet at the German Kaiser, though she succeeded only in damaging his carriage.

Other developments in Germany were more ominous still. On 6 June the Reichstag passed the Germany Navy Bill – a 20 year plan to build 19 battleships, 8 large and 15 small cruisers, at a cost of 861,000,000 marks. And Count Ferdinand von Zeppelin's enormous airship, which was to become such a dominant feature of the First World War, had its maiden flight, rising to a height of 1,000 feet with its inventor on board.

John Heseltine

The Palace of Knossos

The ancient Minoan palace at Knossos on Crete, built around 2000 BC, was excavated in 1900 by Sir Arthur Evans (1851-1941). With its numerous rooms and corridors, the palace had inspired the famous Greek legend of the Labyrinth.

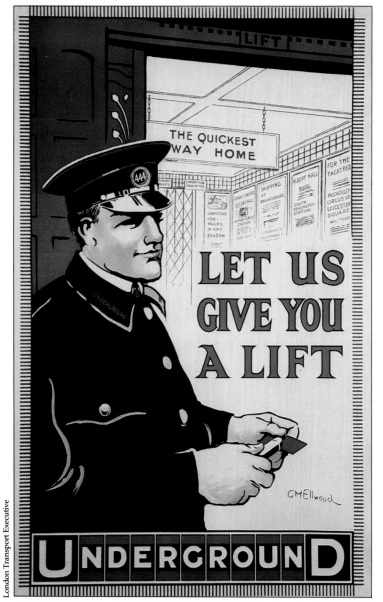

London Transport Executive

National Army Museum

John Heseltine

Browning pistol

The first automatic pistol was manufactured in 1900 by John Moses Browning (1855-1926), who made his first gun from scrap metal at the age of 13 and designed the breech-loading single shot rifle for the Winchester Co.

Gauguin: Self-portrait with *The Yellow Christ* (detail)/Private Collection

G. Gauguin

1848-1903

Paul Gauguin was one of the most revolutionary painters of the 19th century, as unconventional in his art as he was in his lifestyle. At the age of 35 he abandoned a respectable business career to devote himself to painting, and his desire for personal and artistic freedom eventually made him an outcast from society. His final years were spent in the South Seas: poor, ill and often without proper materials for painting.

Gauguin soon reacted against the light-hearted style in which he began his career and turned to weightier subjects. His bold colours and shapes expressed his own inner vision rather than external reality. When he died, Gauguin was virtually forgotten, but an exhibition of his work in Paris three years later revealed his genius, and since then he has been one of the greatest influences on 20th-century art.

Stockbroker in the South Seas

When he became a stockbroker at the age of 23, Gauguin seemed to have settled for a conventional middle-class life. But adventure was in his blood, and 12 years later he risked everything for art.

Colorphoto Hinz

Private Collection

A late starter
The first self-portrait Gauguin painted dates from about 1885, two years after he had abandoned commerce for art in his mid-thirties.

Paul Gauguin was born in Paris on 7 June 1848. His father Clovis was a radical journalist, and there was radical blood on his mother's side, too – Aline was the daughter of the Peruvian-born feminist and socialist Flora Tristan. But the year of Paul's birth was a bad time for radicals. By November 1848, Louis Napoleon had seized power in France, and his political opponents had a tendency to disappear. Clovis decided to visit his wife's relatives, and the family sailed to Peru in 1849.

Clovis died of a heart attack on the journey from France, but Aline, with Paul and his sister Marie, spent the next six years in Lima under the protection of her great-uncle. Then Paul's grandfather died in France, and the family returned to take up their inheritance in the old man's home town of Orleans.

Dull, provincial and thoroughly bourgeois, Orleans was a depressing contrast to colourful, subtropical Peru, and Paul hated it. When he was 17, he did what thousands of restless, adventurous young men had done before him: he went to sea. He worked for three years on a merchant vessel, and when he became due for military service in

Jean-Loup Charmet

The Image Bank/P. Knapp

Gauguin's feminist grandmother
(above) Gauguin's maternal grandmother was the Peruvian-born feminist and socialist, Flora Tristan. Gauguin's father, Clovis, was also a radical, and his political views meant that they had to seek refuge in Peru after Louis Napoleon (the Emperor's nephew) seized power in France in 1848.

Wife and children
Gauguin and his Danish wife Mette had five children during the first ten prosperous years of their marriage. Mette was a strong character who looked after the children when Gauguin abandoned them – with everything else – for his art.

Peruvian childhood
(below) The taste for colourful, exotic places that ran throughout Gauguin's life began with his childhood in Peru. He was taken there by his parents when a baby and lived there for six years with his mother's family.

1868, he chose to serve his stint in the navy.

Paul was released from the service in 1871, and it seemed he had got the taste for adventure out of his system. He was 23, and it was time for him, as a young man of respectable family, to settle down. His mother had died while he was still at sea, but had previously arranged for the wealthy banker Gustave Arosa to be Paul's guardian. Arosa was happy to use his contacts to find him a post with a leading Paris stockbroker.

A BUSINESS CAREER

Gauguin's clerkship was a comfortable, well-paid job, and it gave him plenty of opportunity for lucrative speculation on the stock exchange. An affluent middle-class future seemed assured. In 1873 he married a Danish girl, Mette Sophie Gad, and they progressed from a fine apartment in town to an even finer suburban house, as Mette regularly produced the next generation of Gauguins. By 1883, he had money, a business reputation, a good home and five children.

But Gauguin had developed a hobby – he liked to paint. His interest in art was encouraged by his guardian, who had a fine collection of paintings and in whose house most of the best-known painters of the day appeared from time to time. Gauguin was encouraged also by Arosa's daughter, an amateur painter, and in 1874 he had some lessons with the Impressionist Camille Pissarro. But essentially he was self-taught.

At Arosa's house and elsewhere, Gauguin had met the leading Impressionist painters and even started to buy their work. He began to align

A career in finance
In 1871 Gauguin began work as a clerk with the firm of Bertin, a leading Paris stockbroker. His career flourished for 12 years (he became Bertin's chief assistant), but he resigned to be free 'to paint every day'.

45

Breton faith
Gauguin often worked in Brittany – an isolated region of north-west France. It was a place of ancient traditions and simple faith, and the rugged strength of the people and the landscape appealed to Gauguin. He was particularly inspired by the granite churches, with their medieval carvings.

himself with them, exhibiting in their group shows from 1879 onward. His paintings came in for a fair amount of praise, and they sold quite well. Gauguin must have toyed for some time with the idea of turning professional, but in 1882 his mind was made up for him by a stock-market crash. Gauguin's 'secure' job suddenly looked anything but secure. In 1883, confident of his ability to keep his family by painting, he resigned.

Unfortunately, the general climate of bankruptcy and despondency had much the same effect on the art market as on the stock market. By 1884, Gauguin's savings had run out, he had sold scarcely a painting and although a move from Paris to Rouen in Normandy had reduced his household expenses, his family was fast approaching destitution. Mette now took a hand. Her husband had had a year as a painter and failed; now she insisted the family move to her native Denmark.

DESERTING THE FAMILY

But their move was not a success. Although Gauguin found a job as a sales representative for a manufacturer of tarpaulins, he sold no more of his company's goods than he had of his paintings. Besides, his commitment to his art was now becoming total. Gauguin returned to painting and in 1885 left once more for Paris, leaving Mette with four children in Copenhagen. He took six-year-old Clovis with him.

The following year was perhaps the worst in Gauguin's life. By the winter of 1885-6, he was penniless, and he and his son were reduced to

Gauguin at Pont-Aven

The town of Pont-Aven in Brittany was already a well-known resort of artists when Gauguin first went there in 1886, but today it owes its fame almost entirely to its association with him. Gauguin was too absorbed in his work to take much part in the bohemian social life of the town, but he was respected by the other artists for his strength of character. Between 1886 and 1890 he spent much of his time in Brittany, seeking the seclusion he needed to develop his work.

Roger Viollet

The Bridgeman Art Library

H. de Toulouse-Lautrec/Emile Bernard/Tate Gallery, London

Emile Bernard
Bernard (1868-1941), who had studied in Paris with Lautrec and Van Gogh, worked closely with Gauguin at Pont-Aven in the late 1880s.

The artists' inn
(left) Gauguin – sitting on the kerb, third from the right – poses with fellow artists outside the Pension Gloanec, the favourite hotel for painters.

living in one miserable room. Cold and undernourished, the boy contracted smallpox; to feed him, Gauguin managed to find work as a bill-poster for a railway company. Remarkably, Clovis recovered, but it was the last time Gauguin did anything for his family. From now on, their fate was in Mette's hands.

In June, Gauguin moved once more, to Pont-Aven in Brittany, where he found not only cheap lodging but the company of appreciative fellow-artists. But there was no financial success to match his growing confidence. Returning to Paris at the end of 1886, he almost starved during the winter. The following year, he decided to make a complete break. 'Paris,' he wrote, 'is a desert for a poor man. I must get my energy back, and I'm going to Panama to live like a native.'

Somehow he scraped together the fare, but 'living like a native' in Panama turned out to mean labouring with pick and shovel in the abortive canal project then under way. After a few weeks, sick with fever, he gave up on Panama and ventured to Martinique in the French West Indies. Four months later, ill-health and poverty forced him back to France, and he returned to Brittany.

A VISIT TO VAN GOGH

Creatively, this was a vital period. At the age of 40, he was finding himself at last as a great and original painter. But the Brittany winters depressed him. In October 1888, he accepted an invitation from Vincent van Gogh, whom he had met two years earlier in Paris, to pass the winter

The Panama Canal
In 1887 Gauguin worked as a labourer in a French project to build the Panama Canal, but he caught a fever and was soon forced to give up the work. After a brief visit to the Caribbean island of Martinique he returned to France, ill and penniless.

Tahiti's last king

Gauguin hoped that Pomare V would buy his work, but the king died suddenly before they had a chance to meet – leaving the artist in deep financial trouble.

with him at Arles, in the South of France. But Gauguin had been there only two months when Van Gogh went famously insane, and threatened him with a razor. There was nothing for it but to return to Paris.

Over the next few years, Gauguin alternated between Paris and Brittany, producing some of his best work. His reputation among his contemporaries had never been higher, but he was still desperately short of money, and he had never lost his yearning to return to the tropics. Finally he settled on another French colony – Tahiti – and on 1 April 1891, he sailed from Marseilles.

At first, Tahiti was not what he had hoped for. He got a friendly reception from the Governor, and an audience was arranged for him with the last native king, Pomare V, who Gauguin hoped would prove a source of commissions. But Pomare died suddenly – of drink – a few hours before the audience. Soon Gauguin was disgusted with the capital of Papeete. 'It was Europe all over again,' he wrote, 'just what I thought I had broken away from – made still worse by colonial snobbery.'

In the country district of Mataiea, however, Gauguin found the peace he wanted – and a young Tahitian girl to share his hut. Even in paradise, though, the need for money reared its ugly head. Despite his dreams, Gauguin could not live for free. He lacked the skills to fish or to farm, and in a community of self-sufficient families there was no real possibility of buying food. He had to rely on

Popperfoto

expensive – and incongruous – European canned and dried produce, bought in Papeete. A spell of ill-health made further inroads into his savings, and in 1893 he had to apply to the Governor to have himself repatriated to France.

RETURN TO TAHITI

It was a humiliating return, but the canvases that Gauguin brought back with him persuaded a leading Paris gallery-owner to give him an exhibition. Though sales were poor, Gauguin found himself the centre of the art world's interest. And he had a financial windfall: an uncle back in Orleans died and left him enough money to set up his own studio in Montparnasse. But he was determined to return to Tahiti, and left France for the last time in July 1895.

The eight years that remained to him were great ones for his art, but Gauguin's life was often miserable. Most of the time he was desperately short of money and could rarely afford the stays in

The Image Bank/John Bryson

South Sea paradise

Gauguin sailed to Tahiti in 1891, hoping to find the tropical paradise of his imagination. He spent eight years on the island, painting his greatest works there.

Annah the Javanese

In 1893 Gauguin returned to Paris after his first stay in Tahiti and set up home with Anne Martin, known as Annah the Javanese, 'a superb mulatto with glowing eyes', as a contemporary described her. Gauguin had 'picked her up in Paris', a replacement for the native girl he had left behind in Tahiti. In 1894 Gauguin got into a brawl with some sailors at Concarneau near Pont-Aven when they made fun of Annah, and he broke his ankle. While he was recovering in Brittany – his injury never properly healed – Annah returned to Paris and ransacked his studio. Gauguin never saw her again.

(right) In this portrait, dated 1893, Annah is shown with her pet monkey, which she took everywhere with her. The candour of her pose and expression reveal clearly the pleasure Gauguin took in her physical charms.

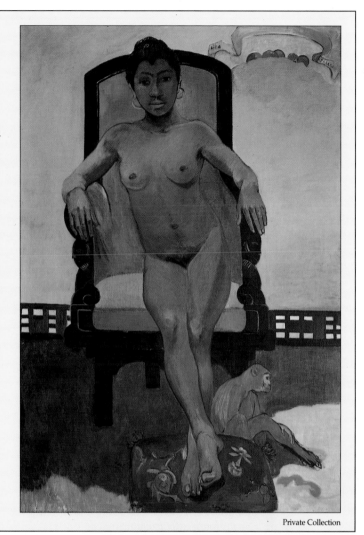

Colorphoto Hinz

Private Collection

Death in the Marquesas
Gauguin spent his last two years in the Marquesas Islands, about 800 miles from Tahiti. His final self-portrait, painted in 1903 – the year he died – shows him facing the end with calm acceptance. His simple grave lies half the globe away from his native France.

hospital that his worsening health – due to syphilis – demanded. In 1897, he even attempted suicide. The following year, he contemplated abandoning painting, and had to take a miserable job as a draughtsman to pay off at least some of his debts.

Disgusted by colonial society and its effects on the Tahitians, Gauguin took to writing vitriolic articles for a local newspaper. In 1901, he abandoned the island altogether and made the 800-mile journey to the Marquesas Islands, where he settled in the village of Atuona. There, he built his last dwelling, 'The House of Pleasure', as he called it. Money at last was coming from Paris, and Gauguin was working happily as well as hard. But he was still making enemies. His attacks on the colonial administration continued and he waged a continuous war with the Catholic Church.

In 1903, the authorities took their revenge. Gauguin was sentenced to three months' imprisonment for 'defamation'. He never served the sentence. On 8 May 1903, aged 54, he died while awaiting the result of an appeal. The local bishop wrote an uncharitable epitaph. 'The only noteworthy event here has been the sudden death of a contemptible individual named Gauguin, a reputed artist, but an enemy of God.' Posterity had a different verdict.

Colorphoto Hinz

Kunstmuseum, Basle

Rapho

Mysteries of Paradise

The exotic culture of the South Sea Islands held a powerful fascination for Gauguin, who chose strange, vivid colours to express the beauty and the mystery he experienced there.

Paul Gauguin was in his early twenties when he took up painting. At first art was no more than a hobby, but he admired and bought the work of the early Impressionists, and based his own style on theirs. As his dedication grew, however, Gauguin soon realized that although these artists, with their bright colours and bold technique, had freed painting from traditional bonds, Impressionism too was limited in scope. Gradually he moved forward to develop the ideas that made him – with Van Gogh and Cézanne – one of the greatest of the Post-Impressionist artists.

The Impressionists had painted the natural world with vividness and directness. But Gauguin was fascinated by ideas more than appearance and wanted his art to express strong emotions: 'Where does the execution of a picture start, where does it end? At the moment when intense feelings are found in the depth of one's being, when they erupt, and thought flows forth like lava from a volcano. Cold and rational calculation have nothing to do with this eruption, for who knows when, in the depths of his being, the work was begun, perhaps unconsciously?'

To express such intensity of feeling, Gauguin had to develop a radically new style of painting.

National Gallery of Scotland, Edinburgh

Martinique Landscape (1887)
(above) After several years painting in the Impressionist manner, Gauguin visited the island of Martinique in the French West Indies. The tropical sunlight triggered a change in his style – he used bolder and brighter colours.

Harvest in Brittany (1889)
This image of peasant women toiling amongst mountainous haystacks was painted at Pont-Aven, in Brittany. From this time onwards, people rather than landscapes dominated Gauguin's canvases.

The Spirit of the Dead Watching (1892)
(right) Gauguin was fascinated by the traditional culture he encountered in Tahiti, and especially by the islanders' spiritual beliefs. The idea for this picture came from a genuine incident: Gauguin returned home from buying lamp oil one night to find his 13-year-old wife Teha'amana lying awake in the dark, terrified of ghosts.

Teha'amana believed that spirits known as tupapaus entered unlighted houses at night. So Gauguin depicted the ghost as Teha'amana would have imagined it – 'like an ordinary little woman stretching out her hand to seize the prey'.

Courtauld Institute Galleries, London

He rejected the idea that a painting had to represent something we can see in the real world, and drew fresh inspiration from non-European art – Gauguin was one of the first artists to take a serious interest in 'primitive' cultures. He spoke of his own 'savage blood', and, perhaps recalling his childhood in Peru, he felt a strong affinity for the vigour of prehistoric Central and South American art. He saw numerous examples of this type of work at the Paris World's Fair of 1889.

REVOLUTIONARY COLOUR

Gauguin also looked for inspiration to Egyptian and Cambodian sculpture, to medieval art and to Japanese prints. He collected postcards of painting and sculpture in a way that is now commonplace among artists and students, but which at the time was novel. In the expressive power of his colour, however, Gauguin went beyond any of his sources. The *Vision after the Sermon* (p.56), one of his most revolutionary paintings, used bright red completely unnaturalistically to set the emotional tone of the painting – one of visionary intensity.

Musée d'Orsay, Paris

Arearea (1892)
(above) This decorative image, with its simplified shapes and intensified colour, evokes the relaxed, unhurried life which Gauguin sought in the South Sea Islands.

Self-Portrait (1889)
(below) Gauguin combined his critical eye and powerful line with a taste for caricature – as in this striking self-portrait. Religious emblems are in generous supply: a halo hovers above Gauguin's head, he holds a snake in his right hand, and the apples of the Garden of Eden hang beside him. These biblical symbols of good, evil and temptation are set in a decorative framework.

National Gallery of Art, Washington

Albright-Knox Art Gallery, Buffalo

The Day of the God (1894)
(left and detail) Gauguin painted this exotic Tahitian scene in Europe, the year before he returned to the South Seas for the last time. The brooding idol and the strange postures of the women summon up the mysteries of Tahitian mythology which so fascinated him. But the beautiful colours are chosen for their decorative as well as expressive effect: the rippling waters of the lagoon form a vivid, abstract pattern.

Art Institute of Chicago

TRADEMARKS

Flat Colour

Unlike the Impressionists, who built up their colours with small dashes of paint, Gauguin used large areas of unbroken colour. When he was painting in Brittany, he often separated these areas with dark lines, but in his Tahitian paintings he sometimes simply butted one area of colour up against another.

Gauguin's Inspiration

'A deep feeling can be interpreted instantly; dream over it, seek its simplest shape.'

'When my wooden clogs echo on this granite, I hear the muffled, heavy and powerful note I am seeking in painting.'

'I have decided on Tahiti . . . and I hope to cultivate my art there in the wild and primitive state.'

The *Vision after the Sermon* was painted at Pont-Aven, where Gauguin briefly inspired a group of like-minded artists. But his personal style reached its fullest flowering in Tahiti. Gauguin's taste for religious and symbolic themes was richly sustained by the native traditions; the bright light produced the strong colours he loved; and the exotic beauty of the islanders made an over-whelming impact on him. He thought that his native models 'possessed something mysterious and penetrating, not beauty in the strict sense of the word. They move with all the suppleness and grace of a sleek animal, giving off that smell which is a mixture of animal odour and the scents of sandalwood and gardenia.'

One of the most characteristic features of Gauguin's work in Tahiti is his use of flat, frieze-

Gauguin's carving
Gauguin was not only a painter – he was also skilled at wood carving, pottery and sculpture. In this boldly executed carving of Eve and the Serpent (1896), he mingles biblical images with obscure Tahitian symbols. The letters PGO are a shortened form of his signature.

Ny Carlsberg Glyptotek, Copenhagen

like compositions, in which he was perhaps influenced by Egyptian art. This kind of composition, in which Gauguin's imposing figures – 'indescribably august and religious in the rhythm of their gestures' – are arranged across the foreground, with little sense of depth, creates a mood of solemn majesty.

Gauguin's technique in the Tahiti paintings was no less distinctive than his composition. Materials were not easily available, so he often had to use coarse sacking rather than proper canvas, spreading his paint thinly to make it go further. From adversity he extracted inspiration, for the limitations of his materials forced him to paint with a rough vigour appropriate to his bold vision.

IMPACT ON MODERN ART

When Gauguin died in 1903, very few people would have agreed with his words in a letter to his wife: 'I am a great artist and I know it. It is because I am, that I have endured such suffering.' Three years after his death, however, 227 of his works were shown in a major exhibition in Paris; this firmly established his reputation among more progressive artists and his subsequent influence on 20th-century art has been immense. The emotional impact of his work and his complete dedication to art – whatever the cost in personal suffering – have made him, like his friend Van Gogh, one of the cult heroes of modern times.

COMPARISONS

Primitive Worlds

Throughout the 19th century, many artists moved away from traditional Western European art to seek new inspiration in ancient cultures. Behind their interest in primitive art lay the desire to create pictures of an innocent world, untouched and uncorrupted by civilized society. Just as Gauguin painted his Tahitian paradise, Hicks and Rousseau created their own visions of unspoilt worlds.

National Gallery, London

The Bridgeman Art Library

Private Collection

Edward Hicks (1780-1849)
The Peaceable Kingdom
A Quaker preacher, Hicks made over 100 versions of his vision of brotherly love.

Henri Rousseau (1844-1910)
Tropical Storm with a Tiger
Rousseau was the most famous of all naïve – untrained – artists, renowned for his jungle fantasies.

Where Do We Come From? What Are We? Where Are We Going To?

Gauguin painted this vast canvas in his Tahitian hut in December 1897. He was in a state of emotional anguish. Depressed by the death of his favourite daughter Aline, he was continually ill with fever and conjunctivitis, and too poor to buy food, let alone medicine. Suicide seemed the only way out. But as he later wrote, 'I wanted to paint a large canvas and put all my energy into it before dying.'

The result was the biggest picture he ever painted – a final testament summing up his ideas about the mysteries of human life. Gauguin worked on the painting 'day and night, at fever pitch' and as soon as he had finished it, tried to poison himself with arsenic. But Gauguin survived. Soon afterwards he wrote to a friend in France explaining the painting's message (summarized, with his own drawings, below right).

The Bridgeman Art Library

Death of a daughter
(right) In March 1897, Gauguin learned that his 20-year old daughter Aline had died in Copenhagen. Although he had abandoned his family years before, he was devastated by the news. 'I have lost a daughter . . . I love God no longer,' he wrote. It was the start of the despair which led to a suicide attempt at the end of the year.

Painted idols
(right) The images of Tahitian gods which appear in Gauguin's paintings are loosely based on Polynesian idols such as this stone carving. The artist made his own interpretations of the island's religious imagery. According to his account, the uplifted arms of the idol in Where Do We Come From? *are pointing out the Beyond – reminding us of the inevitability of death.*

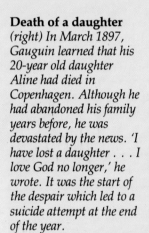

Giraudon

'I can see no way out except death, which delivers us from everything'
Paul Gauguin

Figures from the past
(left) The complex composition of Where Do We Come From? *is, in fact, a combination of several previous paintings. The crouching woman and 'strange white bird' in the left-hand corner also appear in this picture of the legendary character Vairumati, which Gauguin had painted earlier in the year.*

Musée d'Orsay, Paris

Tahitian wildlife
(below) Colourful animals and birds abound in the painting. But it is not certain whether they all have symbolic meanings, or are just exotic details.

Museum of Fine Arts, Boston

The fruit of life
The pivotal figure in Gauguin's allegorical life-cycle reaches up for fruit. Though the action repeats Eve's in the Garden of Eden, the fruit is a mango, not an apple.

Where do we come from?
'On the right at the bottom is a sleeping baby, then three squatting women. Two figures dressed in purple are exchanging thoughts. A crouching figure, deliberately enormous despite the perspective, raises its arms in the air and looks astonished at these two figures who dare to think of their destiny.'

What are we?
'A figure in the centre is picking fruit. Two cats by a child. A white goat. The idol, with arms mysteriously raised, points out the Beyond. The fruit-picking symbolizes the pleasures of life; the fullness of the figure would be happiness unmarred were it not for the idol which is a reminder of eternal truths, a menace forever threatening humanity.'

Where are we going to?
'A squatting figure seems to be listening to the idol. Then an old woman close to death seems to accept and be resigned to her own fate, ending the story. A strange white bird, holding a lizard between its feet, represents the futility of empty words.'

P. Gauguin 1898 Tahiti

Gallery

Gauguin's paintings bear witness to his search for a primitive, spiritual lifestyle. As early as 1886 he had abandoned 'civilized' Paris for the Breton countryside, and his quest continued in the remote South Sea Islands. In 1888, he painted his first mature work, Vision after the Sermon, while living among the peasants of Brittany. Like the

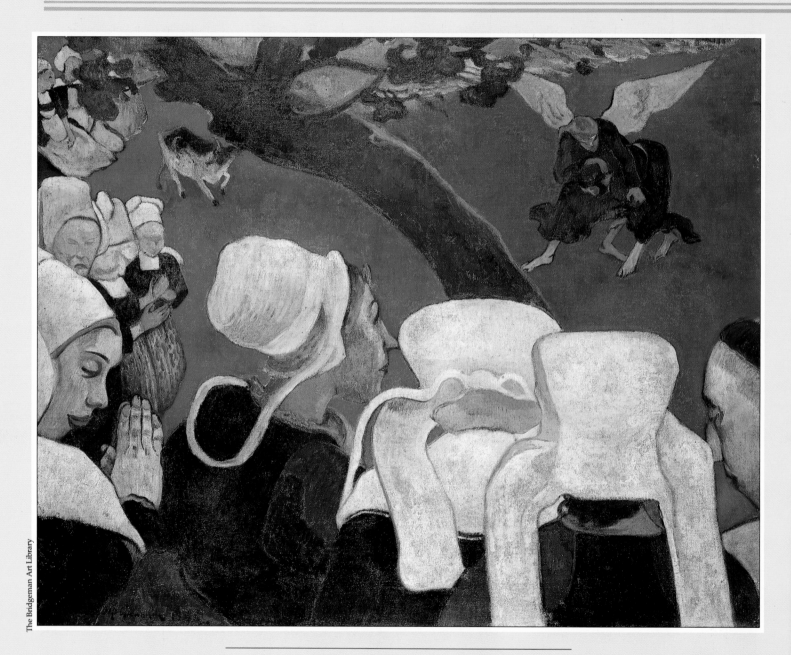

Vision after the Sermon *1888*
28¾″ × 36¼″ National Gallery of Scotland, Edinburgh

In a Breton churchyard, peasant women experience a vision of Jacob — the father of Israel — wrestling with an angel. The Old Testament story may have been the subject of a sermon delivered by the priest who appears on the right. Blending symbol with reality, Gauguin frames the blood-red field of spiritual battle with the women's white headdresses, and separates them from the vision with a tree.

Yellow Christ, it expressed his own feelings about religion in a distinctive, non-realist manner, with bold colours and outlines.

During his first visit to Tahiti, Gauguin painted Girl with a Flower, Women on a Beach and The Market. But he was soon disillusioned by colonial society and left the island for two years.

On his second visit, poverty and disease nearly broke his spirit and the great allegory Where Do We Come From? was intended as a final meditation on life. But Gauguin survived his subsequent attempt at suicide. Late paintings such as The White Horse, and Breasts and Red Flowers show a new-found lyrical harmony.

The Yellow Christ *1889*
36¼" × 28¾"
Albright-Knox Art
Gallery, Buffalo

Peasant women kneel to pray at a wayside crucifix in the Breton countryside. The humanity of the Christ figure expresses just how real the mystic experience is to the women. Yet the colour is totally unreal – the yellow body of Christ and the red trees stress the other-worldliness of the scene. The child-like drawing with its strong black outlines is deliberately reminiscent of medieval stained glass.

Tahitian Girl with a Flower *1891*
27½″ × 18″ Ny Carlsberg Glyptotek, Copenhagen

Gauguin painted his magnificent portrait of a Tahitian girl wearing Western-style clothes soon after his arrival in the South Seas. Despite her grey dress, the girl is linked to the brightly coloured backdrop by the flower which she holds. The Tahitian title appears as part of the decorative scheme.

Giraudon

Two Tahitian Women on a Beach *1891*
27″ × 35¾″ Musée d'Orsay, Paris

Two statuesque women laze on a sandy Tahitian beach, both self-absorbed and silent, in a mood of timelessness and languor. The background is made up of bands of flat colour, which divide up the canvas vertically. This has the effect of pushing the figures forward, emphasizing their monumental solidity.

Giraudon

TA MATETE

Paul Gauguin

P Gauguin

The Market *1892*
28¼" × 36¼" Kunstmuseum, Basle

Gauguin mixes Tahitian with Egyptian imagery in this frieze-like painting, and in fact the composition derives from a photograph of an ancient Egyptian wall-painting. A simple rhythm of turned heads and stylized gestures runs across the canvas as a counterpoint to the girls' bent knees, which are all turned in the same direction. The paint is applied very thinly on the coarse sacking canvas – Gauguin was too poor to be generous with his paint.

**Where Do We Come From? What Are We?
Where Are We Going To?** *1897*
54¾″ × 147½″ Museum of Fine Arts, Boston

*Painted after one of the worst years in Gauguin's life, this 12-foot
canvas was intended to be his parting message to the world. The
painting 'reads' from right to left, beginning with the baby and
moving across to the old woman contemplating death. The questions
of the title – written in the yellow panel in French rather than
Tahitian – remained unanswered and unanswerable.*

The White Horse *1898*
55½″ × 35¾″ Musée d'Orsay, Paris

*A white horse – turned green beneath the tropical leaves – bends to
drink from the rippling blue and orange water of a mountain stream,
while naked men ride bareback through the forest. With lines and
colours exaggerated for emotional effect, this vision of human beings
at one with nature evokes the earthly paradise Gauguin sought.*

Breasts and Red Flowers *1899*
37" × 28¾" Metropolitan Museum of Art, New York

*In this graceful painting of two Tahitian women with an offering of
mango flowers, a gentle curve sweeps down the white dress and
through the bowl, linking the girls' breasts, while the off-centre
composition provides a sense of movement. The lyrical calm of this
work belies the fact that Gauguin was racked by illness at the time.*

The Lure of Tahiti

The jewel of the vast Pacific Ocean, Tahiti was famed as a paradise on earth long before Gauguin visited its shores. European sailors had savoured the island's pleasures since the days of Captain Cook.

In 1890, Gauguin wrote to a friend 'I am leaving for Tahiti, where I shall hope to end my days.' His decision was influenced partly by the fact that Tahiti was as far away from Paris as it was possible to get, but also by the stream of enthusiastic reports reaching Europe from travellers who had visited the hauntingly beautiful island.

The unspoiled paradise of Gauguin's dreams, however, had vanished long before he reached the capital Papeete in 1891. There were church bells and gendarmes awaiting him as well as lovely garlanded maidens, stolid French housewives preparing old-fashioned country meals as well as carefree islanders living free off taro, yam and breadfruit. The 'mysterious beings' he had imagined before his arrival managed to consume 45,000 gallons of island rum and 65,000 gallons of imported claret each year.

But the place itself was too lovely and the people too resilient for either to be spoiled completely. Communications were so bad that Europeanized Papeete could not make much of an

John Webber/James Cook/National Portrait Gallery, London

Mutiny on the Bounty
The ignominious fate of Captain Bligh – cast adrift from his own ship in April 1789 – was powerful evidence of the lure of Tahiti. Fletcher Christian and his co-mutineers returned to the island before founding their own colony, with Tahitian wives, on Pitcairn Island.

The Fotomas Index

impression on the rest of the island. Even today the only real road follows the coast, and in the 1890s, the interior was largely trackless. In rural districts, people lived much as they always had, by fishing or small-scale farming.

AN EXTINCT VOLCANO

Tahiti had a mesmerizing effect on Gauguin, as it had on other European visitors since its discovery by Britain's Captain Samuel Wallis in 1767. An extinct volcano lost in the immensity of the South Pacific, its lush, green slopes rise to a 7,349-foot peak, high above a shoreline ringed by coral reefs that enclose lagoons swarming with fish. But it was the island's inhabitants who made the greatest impression on the early explorers. They were handsome and easy-going people, Polynesians whose ancestors had settled around 4,000 years ago. In Tahiti they had evolved a life-style that Westerners, accustomed to the drudgery of their own societies, saw as a kind of paradise.

The climate, though a little damp, was balmy and reasonably cool by tropical standards. Fish and shellfish, breadfruit and bananas seemed to be had for the asking, without labour. There was little need for clothing. And as Wallis and his crew discovered – to the captain's horror and the men's delight – the languid young women of the island were only too willing to exchange their favours for some trifling gift. Iron nails were the favoured currency: by the time Wallis sailed for home after a month's sojourn, the fixed bayonets of his Royal Marines were barely enough to stop his men prising out every iron fastening in the ship.

While Wallis, a tough but unimaginative officer, was preparing his report for the Admiralty, an explorer with a more philosophical turn of mind was making his landfall on Tahiti. Louis Antoine de Bougainville was not only a soldier and a navigator. He was also steeped in the new ideas sweeping 18th-century Europe. And in Tahiti he found a reality to match philosopher Jean-Jacques Rousseau's ideal of the noble savage – of man at peace with nature.

Bougainville and his crew were welcomed as Wallis had been. 'They pressed us to choose a woman and to come on shore with her,' he wrote, 'and their gestures, which were unmistakably clear, denoted in what manner we should form an acquaintance with her.' His naturalist, Philibert Commerson, enthused about 'natural man, who is born essentially good, free of every prejudice, and who follows, without defiance and without remorse, the gentle impulses of instinct not yet corrupted by reason.'

WARRIOR SOCIETY

Commerson's was a notion that endured until Gauguin's time and after. But although it contained a germ of truth, it was largely illusion born out of wishful thinking. For life on Tahiti was no idyll. The islanders did not use the leisure time granted by their comfortable environment to live the kind of rapturous, untrammelled existence dreamed of by European philosophers. Instead, with or without assistance from 'the gentle impulses of instinct', they had created a fierce warrior society that indulged in slavery and human sacrifice.

Nor did the blithe promiscuity of many young Tahitian women mean that they were devotees of free love. In fact, the Tahitians had a complex set of rules for sexual behaviour inside and outside marriage, which even today anthropologists have not fully elucidated. A European who made an enthusiastic grab for the wrong woman could –

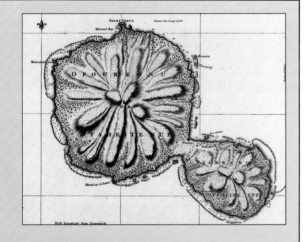

Captain Cook charts Tahiti
James Cook – one of England's greatest explorers – visited Tahiti in 1769 on board the Endeavour, *and produced this early chart of the island.*

Matavai Bay
With its wonderful natural harbour at Matavai Bay, the island of Tahiti became the centre for early voyages to Polynesia. This picture, painted in 1773 by William Hodges, Captain Cook's artist on his second voyage, shows Cook's ships, HMS Resolution *and HMS* Adventure *in the bay.*

Roger Viollet

The Royal Family
*An early photograph
shows the Royal Family in
Western-style clothing
outside their residence on
the island of Ra'iatea.
Before the advent of
Christianity, the nearby
island had been Tahiti's
centre of worship.*

Princess Poedua
*Poedua was a Ra'iatean
princess, painted in 1777
by Cook's artist on HMS*
Resolution *John Webber.
She epitomizes the beauty
of Tahitian women:
delicate tatoos decorate her
arms, and in her right
hand she holds a fly whisk.*

John Webber/Poedua/National Maritime Museum, London

and often did – pay for it with his life.

Nevertheless, the island never lost its seductive fascination. Captain James Cook, who visited it in 1769, was reduced to holding Tahitian chiefs hostage to obtain the return of deserters from his ship – and Cook was a well-loved leader. In 1789, the contrast between Tahitian life and Royal Naval discipline was enough to provoke the celebrated mutiny on HMS *Bounty*. Regardless of its flaws, paradise Tahiti-style was better than life on ship.

But the coming of the Europeans was itself enough to put an end to the old way of life. The newcomers brought syphilis, a poor return for the island women's affections. They brought measles and smallpox and a host of other diseases to which the Polynesians had little or no resistance. They brought rum. And unscrupulous and well-armed Europeans took sides for their own advantage in the island's internal quarrels, which were bloody enough already without their help.

DESTRUCTION OF A PEOPLE

The results were quite devastating. According to some estimates, Tahiti's 402 square miles supported as many as 150,000 people before the Europeans came. By the end of the century the population had crashed to 15,000; by 1830 it had fallen to 8,000.

Missionaries did their own kind of damage. Their first settlement was established in 1797, and although they did their best to protect their flocks from the ravages of drink and disease, they eventually succeeded in undermining the local traditions that any society needs in order to keep its self-respect. The islanders were told of the evils of nakedness and fornication, and introduced to the doctrinal distinctions between Calvinists and Catholics and all the other Christian sects.

Outright colonization followed. Anglo-French rivalry ended with a half-hearted French Protectorate established in 1843; the last Tahitian king with any pretence at independence abdicated in 1880 and in that year the island became a full French colony.

Tahiti's fate could have been much worse. By 19th-century standards, the colonial administration was efficient and humane. Outside the capital of Papeete, French was seldom spoken, and disputes were more likely to be settled by ancient tribal law than official regulations. Christianity had successfully driven out the old pagan worship, and even the names of ancient gods had been forgotten; but although Tahitians had become regular church-goers, traditional festivals of song and dance had survived.

A cold observer would see that imported, factory-woven cloth had replaced native products, that there was much hymn-singing, that bit by bit the population was beginning to drift towards the modestly bright lights of Papeete. But a painter would see what his mind wanted to see. Paradise, like beauty, was in the eye of the beholder.

The Fotomas Index

War galleys

Despite their friendliness to Europeans, the Tahitians were formidable in battle. Their war galley – called a pahi *– was deep-keeled with a fighting platform. Battle chiefs wore flamboyant dress and high headdresses to impress and terrify the enemy.*

Bearing gifts

British seamen arriving at Tahiti soon learned that the beautiful island women were usually only too pleased to exchange their favours for gifts. But approaching the wrong woman could be very dangerous, and even result in death.

Powerful idols

(below) Tahitian religion centred on the worship of gods and ancestral spirits and could involve human sacrifice. Sorcerers used wooden images, known as ti'i, *when mobilizing the spirits to harm their enemies.*

William Hodges/War Canoes/National Maritime Museum, London

John Hillelson Agency/Bruno Barbey/Magnum

A Year in 1889
the Life

The collapse of the Panama Canal scheme, on which Gauguin himself had worked as a labourer, was the worst financial scandal to hit France for centuries. Austria too was rocked by scandal, when the Crown Prince committed suicide with his lover. And in London, dock workers made history with a famous strike for wages of sixpence an hour.

Jean-Loup Charmet

Aldus Archive

Paying for the Canal

(right) The French scheme for building a canal through the isthmus of Panama collapsed in 1889. It was underfinanced and mismanaged from the start, and the work force was decimated by yellow fever. The isthmus became a centre of gambling, brothel keeping – and coffin making. The US Government took up the project in 1904, but used only one-third of the French excavations. They finally completed the canal in 1914.

Blood transfusions

Early experiments used animal blood – always fatally – for transfusions. In 1889 Georges Hayem (1841-1933) made crucial progress in defining human blood groups.

Back-wheel drive

René Panhard (1841-1908) and Emile Levassor (d.1897) produced the first car with an internal combustion engine mounted at the front, and a clutch and transmission to carry power to the rear wheels. The prototype was completed by 1889.

Archiv fur Kunst und Geschichte

The Mayerling scandal

(left) In January, Rudolf of Austria and his mistress Marie died in a double suicide at Mayerling. To avoid scandal, the bodies were removed separately by night. Maria was buried surreptitiously nearby, while the Prince was taken to the imperial palace to lie in state before the funeral.

For the Vicomte Ferdinand Marie de Lesseps – promoter of the Suez Canal, diplomat, entrepreneur and a distinguished member of the French establishment – 1889 was a disastrous year. His latest scheme, to build a sea-level canal across the isthmus of Panama from the Atlantic to the Pacific, had collapsed around his ears. In February, the Panama Canal Company revealed debts of more than £60,000,000 and an official investigation exposed a vast scandal.

SHORTAGE OF FUNDS

There had been problems from the start, seven years earlier, for the Panama enterprise was hampered by a drastic shortage of funds. De Lesseps had underestimated the cost of the canal and asked for only 300 million francs. When work began there was mismanagement in the allocation of contracts, the design of the machinery and the organization of the work. Yellow fever killed off European workers as fast as they were sent out, and debilitated the survivors. Two years earlier Gauguin himself had worked on the Canal, but was forced to leave after a few weeks, racked with disease.

To keep the work going at all, it had been essential to find more money, and such was De Lesseps' reputation that thousands of small investors – cab drivers, shop-keepers, peasants – had poured their savings into the venture. But the problems continued to grow. Despite the importance of the enterprise for French prestige, the government refused any financial support until December 1888, when an issue of lottery

The Mansell Collection

bonds was finally authorized. And when these proved undersubscribed, the company had no choice but to go bankrupt in February 1889. It was the greatest financial disaster in France for nearly 200 years.

The government tried to hush up the scandal, but eventually De Lesseps and some of his associates were put on trial. The enquiry revealed that financial control of the company was exercised by two Jews with dubious reputations but high political connections. These revelations caused the government grave embarrassment and fuelled the flames of anti-semitism in France. De Lesseps was arrested, convicted of misappropriating funds, and sentenced to five years in jail. But in the event, his punishment was restricted to public humiliation as the verdict was later quashed.

The same year the doomed Habsburg Empire of Austria and Hungary was also rocked by scandal. Crown Prince Rudolph, heir to Emperor Franz Joseph, shot himself through the head with a revolver on 29 January at Mayerling, a shooting lodge in the wooded hills some 20 miles from Vienna. Next to his body was found that of 17-year-old Baroness Marie Vetsera, the niece of a rich Levantine banker – and a ravishing 'oriental' beauty. It was a suicide pact. But what was the motive?

SON AGAINST FATHER

Rumours of a family conflict were rife throughout Europe. The Prince, though a dreamer, was known to be at odds with his father's policy of appeasing Russia, their powerful

A victory for Ethiopia
In 1889, during the 'Scramble for Africa', Italy sought to colonize Ethiopia. The Emperor Menelik II concluded the Treaty of Ucciali with the Italians, but later denounced its wording. The Italians invaded, but were repulsed in 1896. A contemporary cartoon shows Menelik treating the Italians gently after their defeat.

The Paris Exhibition
The 1889 International Exhibition in Paris displayed all the latest technology and attracted 2,500,000 visitors. The most spectacular exhibits were a large-scale model of the Earth – and the Eiffel Tower, completed that year.

neighbour. Moreover, Rudolph's marriage to Stephanie, daughter of Leopold II of Belgium, was not a success. It had been arranged by the Emperor and Rudolph took refuge in drink, drugs and love affairs.

The Prince wrote farewell letters to his wife and mother, but not a word to his father. Their contents have never been revealed, but it seems that Rudolph was mentally unbalanced, seized by a romantic vision of death. He probably felt himself to be a failure, unable to translate his vision into political action when he saw his father's character and policy leading the Empire to disaster.

But 1889 saw triumphs as well as tragedies. Gustave Eiffel, who designed the locks for the Panama Canal, had his greatest success on 31 March when he saw his 1,000 foot cast-iron tower inaugurated in Paris. The tower cost some £240,000 to build and weighed 7,000 tons. A spiral iron staircase of 1,600 steps ran up the centre of the tower, but most visitors found this too vertigo-inducing and preferred to take the lift, which took seven minutes to reach the summit.

THE PARIS INTERNATIONAL EXHIBITION

The Eiffel Tower was to prove the principal attraction of the Paris International Exhibition opened by the President of the Republic, Sadi Carnot, on 6 May. The Exhibition ran until 6 November, displaying the industrial and commercial wealth of France, and attracted 2,500,000 visitors. But 1889 was also the centenary of the French Revolution and the spirit of rebellion

The Rescue of Emin Pasha
Henry Stanley's last African expedition was to rescue Emin Pasha, governor of Egypt's Equatorial Province, who had been cut off from the outside world by rebels. Stanley left England in 1887, and found Emin near Lake Albert the next year. They arrived at the coast near Zanzibar in December 1889. Stanley's In Darkest Africa *(1890) is an account of this arduous journey.*

Settlers in Oklahoma
Following a treaty between the Creek and Seminole Indians and the US Government, Oklahoma was declared open to white settlement on 22 April 1889. That day, thousands of settlers crossed the border and by nightfall a tented 'Oklahoma City' had been built.

Aldus Archive

was aroused. When the President left his official residence at the Elysée Palace to drive by carriage to the Palace of Versailles, a disaffected, anti-Republican storekeeper named M. Perrin fired a revolver at him. But the cartridges were blank and the President was able to proceed to Versailles unharmed.

LONDON'S DOCK STRIKE

In London, political events were less flamboyant, but their influence was longer-lasting. In August and September, Ben Tillet led the London dockers in their famous strike to demand 'the docker's tanner' – a wage of just 6d an hour. The dockers' leaders were skilful in stirring up popular opinion and £4,500 was raised by general subscription. By the end of the year, their

union numbered 30,000 members: evidence of the now rapid growth of unionism among semi-skilled and unskilled workers.

Not far from the docks, in the East End streets around Whitechapel, 'Jack the Ripper' continued his grisly business. In July the body of a women called Mackenzie was found brutally murdered and, at dawn on 10 September, a policeman found a mutilated female torso under a railway arch in Whitechapel.

In December, the year ended in triumph for the explorer Henry Morton Stanley who finally reached Zanzibar. But for Charles Parnell, the hero of Irish nationalism, 1889 ended in despair. He was cited in divorce proceedings by Captain O'Shea, the husband of his mistress Katherine. In Catholic Ireland, the disgrace finished Parnell's career, and the campaign for Irish Home Rule lost its most valuable leader.

National Museum of Labour History

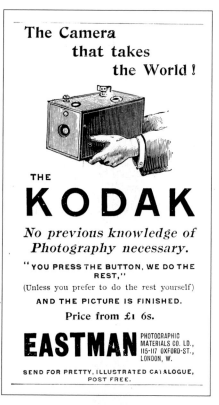

Mary Evans Picture Library

The first Kodak camera
Kodak No. 1, the first portable roll film camera, went on sale in 1888, but the roll film was not perfected until the following year. Each time a film was used up, the whole camera was returned to the manufacturer – the Eastman company – who printed the pictures and reloaded the camera.

The London Dock Strike
In their famous battle for the 'Dockers' Tanner', dock workers came out on strike in 1889 for a wage of sixpence an hour. Support strikes were organized by numerous other workers, including jam and dog-biscuit makers. The strike ended exactly a month after it began, with the dockers winning their 'tanner' and their union gaining new strength.

Van Gogh: Self-portrait, aged 35/National Museum Vincent van Gogh, Amsterdam

Vincent
1853-1890

One of the most original artists ever, Vincent van Gogh worked as an evangelist before taking up painting at the age of 27. He was largely self-taught, but absorbed the inspiring lessons of Impressionism during two years in Paris. Then he moved alone to Arles in the south of France, where he painted the landscapes, still-lifes and portraits which became his most famous works. They are all signed simply 'Vincent'.

Van Gogh's life was a grim and desperate struggle against poverty, hunger, alcoholism and insanity. His attempt to found an artist's colony with the painter Paul Gauguin ended in the harrowing experience of self-mutilation, when he cut off part of his left ear. And though his younger brother Theo supported him to the last, Vincent's agony ended in suicide. He shot himself in the chest, aged 37.

Dutchman with a Mission

The son of a protestant minister, Vincent van Gogh worked as an evangelist before turning to art at the age of 27. He bought the same zeal to painting until his tragic suicide 10 years later.

Vincent Willem van Gogh was born on 30 March 1853 in the small Dutch village of Groot Zundert, near the Belgian frontier. He was the first surviving son of the local pastor, Theodorus van Gogh, and his wife Cornelia, a gentle, artistic woman. By an extraordinary coincidence, the boy was born exactly one year to the day after Cornelia had delivered a stillborn baby, also called Vincent Willem.

The grieving parents had placed a gravestone in the village churchyard for their lost infant, so little Vincent grew up with a constant reminder of his dead namesake. He was a difficult child, who spent his time walking alone in the fields, rarely playing even with his younger brother Theo or his three little sisters. There is no record of his school career, but – encouraged by his mother – he drew and painted regularly from his early teens.

One of Vincent's uncles was a successful art dealer with a business in the Hague which he had merged with the Paris-based international firm of Goupil & Co. When Vincent left school at the age

The Dutch landscape
(below) Van Gogh was born near the Dutch-Belgian border – a flat land of heath and peat bogs.

of 16, Uncle Cent found him a job in the Hague office, and he worked there steadily for four years, with a short stint in the Brussels branch. But this period of calm was not to last. In 1873 Vincent was transferred to London, where he fell disastrously in love with his landlady's daughter. This affair affected his ability to work and he was dismissed.

In 1876 Van Gogh returned to England as an unpaid assistant at a private school in Ramsgate. After a few months the school moved to London,

Van Gogh at 13
The eldest of six children – three boys and three girls – Vincent was a solitary child who spent long hours walking in the countryside.

Groot Zundert church
Near the door of his father's church stood the tombstone of Vincent's still-born elder brother, who had the same birthday and the same name.

and he was given the job of collecting overdue school fees in some of the city's poorest areas. It was his first real view of urban squalor and what he saw so distressed him that he could not bring himself to collect a penny. He soon resigned.

But the experience of poverty awakened a religious zeal in Van Gogh, who now followed his father's example by becoming an assistant preacher to a Methodist minister. He enjoyed this work enormously, and after a few months he returned to Holland to train formally for the ministry. Vincent's parents doubted that he had the self-discipline to cope with the rigorous studies required. They were right: he gave up after a year. But his passion was unchecked and at the age of 25 he moved to the Borinage, a grim coal-mining district in southern Belgium, as an evangelist.

A GIFT TO THE POOR

The poverty Vincent found there was even worse than in London. He threw himself into his work with a selfless fervour, interpreting Christ's message to 'give to the poor' so literally that he even gave his warm clothes away, and ate almost nothing. His superiors were appalled by his 'excessive' zeal. They were also dismayed by his appearance, which they felt brought disrespect on his calling. Once again, Vincent was dismissed.

Despite the loss of his job, Van Gogh remained in the Borinage for two hard years, surviving no-one knew how. And there he went through a profound personal crisis to emerge with a new resolve: to be an artist.

He went home to his parents and applied himself to the task with the same vigour he had

The artist's parents
Theodorus van Gogh, the pastor of Groot Zundert, was a pious man who encouraged his son's religious leanings, but Vincent's passionate evangelism provoked many arguments between them. His wife Cornelia, a bookbinder's daughter, was related to painters and art dealers. She painted watercolours before her marriage.

Key Dates

1853 born in Groot Zundert, Holland

1869 goes to work for art dealers Goupil and Co. in The Hague

1873 transferred to London, but dismissed

1876 returns to England as an unpaid school teacher. Resigns to become an assistant Methodist preacher in London

1877 returns home

1878 moves to Belgian mining district as an evangelist

1880 decides to become an artist

1885 paints *The Potato Eaters*

1886 moves in with brother Theo in Paris

1888 moves to Arles, South of France. Paints *Sunflowers*, *Bedroom at Arles*. Joined by painter Paul Gauguin

1889 commits himself to St Rémy mental asylum

1890 moves to Auvers, village north of Paris. Shoots himself fatally

Mission to the miners
At the age of 25, Van Gogh went as a missionary to the Borinage district of Belgium. There he made his decision to be an artist.

Vincent's Lost Loves

Throughout his life, Van Gogh was plagued by loneliness. He never married, and his few attempts to find happiness with women all ended disastrously. Vincent's first love affair was with his landlady's daughter in England: it disturbed him so much that he lost his job. The second was with Kee Vos, his widowed cousin who was staying with his parents in Holland. Scared by ardent protestations of love for her, she fled to Amsterdam.

He still craved a loving relationship, and when he met a pregnant prostitute called Sien in The Hague, he saw it as his mission to give her love and protection. Vincent lived with Sien and her children, revelled in his 'family life', and planned to marry her. But the unlikely couple parted after a year.

(right) Vincent's mistress Sien modelled for this picture of Sorrow, which shows her pregnant and alone, as she was when he found her.

(right) Vincent fell in love with his cousin Kee Vos when she was staying with his parents. Recently widowed, she rejected his advances.

National Museum Vincent van Gogh, Amsterdam

brought to evangelism. For months he was happier than ever before, and his work improved rapidly. But ominous signs of instability revealed themselves in his stormy behaviour. Another abortive love affair shook him badly; then a religious quarrel with his father reached such a pitch that Vincent walked out of the house on Christmas Day 1881, and moved to The Hague.

With no money to live on, he was forced to ask Theo for help. His loyal brother sent him a tiny allowance each month from his own small salary – in the spirit of self-sacrifice that would endure throughout Vincent's life. Meanwhile the landscape artist Anton Mauve (a relation of Van Gogh's mother) encouraged his painting until a typical outburst brought their friendship to an end. Defiantly, Vincent shared his room with a prostitute and her small child, and even talked of marriage until Theo persuaded him to drop the plan.

PORTRAITS OF PEASANTS

Vincent returned home in 1884. His parents had moved to a new church in Nuenen; they welcomed him like a prodigal son. He began to work on portraits of peasants and after yet another emotional disaster he executed his most ambitious picture so far: *The Potato Eaters* (p.82), a gloomy painting of peasants at their evening meal.

Pastor Theodorus died in 1885, and the same year Van Gogh left Holland, never to return. He went first to Belgium and enrolled at the academy in Antwerp, but failed his first term of study. By the time the results were declared, he had already left for Paris. One day Theo – still working for Goupil's – received a brief note urging him to 'come to the Salle Carrée (in the Louvre) as soon as possible,' where his brother was waiting.

Van Gogh in Paris
In 1886 Vincent moved to Paris, where he shared a flat with his brother Theo in the village suburb of Montmartre. There he met and painted with other artists – including Toulouse-Lautrec and Gauguin – but two years of hard work and heavy drinking took a severe toll of his health. This self-portrait, showing him thin and drawn, was painted in 1887.

The move to Arles
(below) Vincent left Paris in 1888 for Arles, near Marseilles. He worked there alone for nine months, before persuading Gauguin to join him.

National Museum Vincent van Gogh, Amsterdam

Vincent moved into Theo's flat in Montmartre and studied for a few months at the studio of an academic painter named Fernand Cormon, along with Emile Bernard and Toulouse-Lautrec. All three soon broke with Cormon, who was hostile to the new Impressionist movement, led by Monet, Renoir and Degas. But Vincent was inspired by the colour of their paintings, and their habit of working in the open air. Through Theo, he met Camille Pissarro, one of the elder Impressionists, and a still more revolutionary figure: Paul Gauguin.

DEPARTURE FOR THE SOUTH

But while Vincent's art progressed rapidly, he stuck out like a sore thumb among the urbane Parisian artists. He drank very heavily; he had a quick, unpredictable temper; he shouted when excited about something; and was incapable of either hiding his opinions or softening them to avoid arguments. He even managed to alienate Theo, but only for a time. After two years in Paris he declared 'I will take myself off somewhere down south.'

In Paris, Vincent had come to like Japanese art and this influenced his choice of where to live. As

Spectrum Colour Library

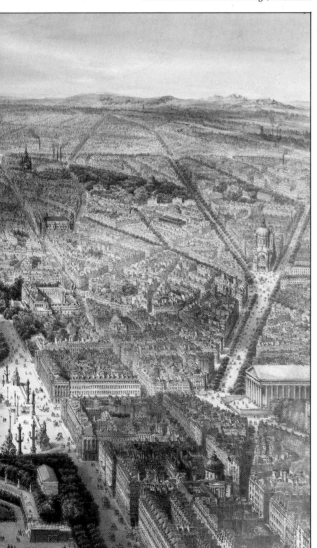

Paris and Montmartre
Paris in the 1880s was one of Europe's grandest cities, with the magnificent new avenue of the Champs Elysées stretching from the Place de la Concorde (bottom) to the Arc de Triomphe. But the centre of the art world was Montmartre, situated in the hills to the north of the city.

Private Collection

he imagined the south of France to be the French equivalent of Japan, he moved to Arles – a provincial city near Marseilles. He arrived by train in February 1888 to find the town covered in snow.

When spring came, he rented a two-storied house in the Place Lamartine. The outside walls were yellow – symbolic of friendship in Japanese culture. He was delighted with the Yellow House, and plunged into his work in a mood of rare happiness, bordering on ecstasy. 'Ideas,' he wrote to Theo, 'are coming to me in swarms.'

Vincent's strange appearance and behaviour caused some derision among the townspeople, but he struck up a genuine friendship with the postman Roulin and his family, a local café owner and a lieutenant from the army.

As usual Van Gogh was overworking, but he felt secure and full of hope. He felt ready to

The Asylum at St Rémy

Van Gogh entered the mental asylum at St Rémy, near Arles, in May 1889. For six months he had suffered recurring bouts of convulsions and hallucinations which terrified him. The doctors gave him little treatment other than cold baths, but allowed Vincent to go out and paint during his periods of calm.

embark on a project he had long desired: the establishment of an artists' colony. He wanted Paul Gauguin to be the first to join, and enlisted Theo to help persuade him. Gauguin – then working in Brittany – was reluctant at first, but when Theo offered to pay his fare, he finally agreed.

GAUGUIN IN ARLES

Gauguin arrived at Arles in October 1888 and moved into the Yellow House, but he disliked the town and found Vincent's untidiness irritating. For a short time peace reigned, but within two months the artists were quarrelling fiercely. Cynical and arrogant, Gauguin made a bad match for the passionate, obstinate Dutchman. Van Gogh was soon making excuses to Theo for their lack of concord, predicting sadly that Gauguin would 'definitely go, or else definitely stay' and claiming to await his decision with 'absolute serenity'.

But the very night he wrote these words, in Christmas week, 1888, something happened to snap Vincent's self-control. He threw a glass of absinthe at Gauguin, and later threatened him with a razor. Gauguin took shelter in a nearby hotel, leav-

Gauguin comes to Arles

In October 1888, Gauguin arrived in Arles for a short-lived, but disastrous collaboration with Van Gogh. The two men argued fiercely, and Gauguin fled to Paris at Christmas when Vincent threatened to attack him with a razor – which he finally used on himself.

ing him to calm down. But during the night Van Gogh cut off the lobe of his left ear, then put it in an envelope and gave it to a prostitute.

Gauguin left for Paris by the first available train; Vincent – suffering from hallucinations as well as loss of blood – was taken to Arles hospital. He was released after two weeks, but overwork and a terror of madness brought on a relapse. He went back into hospital. When he recovered enough to go back to the Yellow House, he was persecuted by the townspeople, 80 of whom signed a petition saying that the 'madman' should be put away.

By the spring of 1889, when Vincent had been in Arles for a year, all his hope had gone. The artists colony had come to nothing. Gauguin had vanished. His friend Roulin had been transferred

Courtauld Institute Galleries, London

Vincent's breakdown
*Overwhelmed with remorse after attacking Gauguin,
Van Gogh cut off a piece of his own ear and gave it to a
prostitute. The next day he was committed to Arles
hospital. The nightmare of insanity, from which he
would never fully recover, had begun.*

to another town. Vincent dreaded the return of his
insanity so much that in May he left Arles and
committed himself voluntarily to an asylum in the
nearby town of Saint Rémy.

Slowly he began to come to terms with his illness – perhaps a form of epilepsy, schizophrenia,
or the result of brain damage at birth. He received
no treatment except cold baths twice a week. Bouts
of convulsions and hallucinations recurred in a
three-monthly cycle, but he still produced some
200 canvases during his year in the asylum.

In the spring of 1890 Theo reported hopeful
signs that Vincent's work was at last being recognized. In February, a painting of an Arles vineyard
was sold for 400 francs in a Brussels exhibition. It
was the only canvas Van Gogh ever sold.

Vincent's Devoted Brother

Throughout his troubled life, Vincent received
loyal support from his devoted younger brother,
Theo van Gogh. While working as an art dealer
in Paris, Theo shared his flat with Vincent for
two years; he sent money and art supplies to his
brother in Arles and St Rémy; and gave
him constant encouragement. The effort
may have cost him his life, for six
months after Vincent's death Theo
died of a stroke, leaving a newly-
married wife and a baby son – also
named Vincent.

*(far left) Theo van Gogh in Paris in 1887
(left) A letter from Vincent. For years
the brothers corresponded every week.*

DEATH IN AUVERS

It was time to leave the South. Vincent's old friend
Camille Pissarro suggested he move to Auvers, a
village northwest of Paris which was popular with
artists. So Vincent spent a few days with Theo and
his new wife – and their baby son, named Vincent
Willem after his uncle – then caught the train to
Auvers. There he was placed in the care of Dr
Gachet, an amiable eccentric.

Vincent painted steadily, and seemed at first to
be healthy and in good spirits. He took a small
room in a café, and kept regular hours. But early in
July a trip to visit Theo in Paris caused him great
anxiety. Theo was worried about money – and the
cost of supporting Vincent was very high.

On Sunday 27 July 1890, Van Gogh walked out
of Auvers into the countryside. He returned late in
the evening, went straight up to his room and lay
on the bed. He had shot himself in the chest. All
that night he lay awake, smoking his pipe; the next
day Theo arrived, alerted by Dr Gachet. All
through Monday his friends watched over him,
until at one o'clock in the morning he died in his
brother's arms. He was 37.

Death in Auvers
*Vincent's last home was
this café at Auvers,
northwest of Paris, where
he lived for six weeks from
20 May until 27 July
1890. That Sunday he
walked off into the fields
and shot himself in the
chest, then staggered
home to die in his small
upstairs room.*

A Race against Time

Van Gogh only painted for the last few years of his life, but his output was enormous. He produced more than 800 canvases – working day and night, as if aware of the short time allotted to him.

When Van Gogh took the fateful decision to devote himself to art, in the bleak coal-mining district of the Borinage in Belgium, he was already 27. He had enjoyed sketching since childhood, especially views of the flat Dutch countryside, with peasants labouring in the fields. But he had never learned to paint in oils.

At first he concentrated on drawing, employing a teach-yourself method of the time known as the

of-doors – and he soon abandoned the sombre browns and blacks he had used in Holland for paintings such as *The Potato Eaters*. In Paris, too, he was inspired by Japanese art, which had recently become popular: hundreds of wood-cut prints were readily available at a couple of francs apiece.

Vincent saw Arles as a French version of Japan, and he travelled south in 1888 as if on a personal mission to create a new movement in art. For over

The Painter on his Way to Work 1888
(below) Van Gogh sets out with his easel, canvas and paints to work in the blazing sunshine of southern France. He often completed a picture in a single day.

Dutch peasants
The dark masterpiece of Van Gogh's early period, The Potato Eaters *(left) is coloured 'like a dusty potato'. It shows Vincent's concern for the hard life of the Dutch peasant, and his respect for the dignity of labour – which is also shown in* Peasant Woman *(below), drawn in the same year, 1885. When Vincent went to Paris a year later his painting changed completely, influenced by the Impressionists.*

National Museum Vincent van Gogh, Amsterdam

Bargues technique. He was very conscious of his deficiencies, and eagerly associated with other painters, among them his relative Anton Mauve, whom he visited in the Hague. But Vincent's fierce independence and stormy temperament made it impossible for him to be a pupil – he invariably argued with his mentors.

WORKING OUT OF DOORS

In Paris, he was inspired by the works of the Impressionists and their followers, who had abandoned the methods of traditional art. Working out of doors instead of in the studio, they ignored the idea of a 'finished' painting, in which all colours were mixed on the palette to the correct shade, then laid down smoothly on the canvas and finally varnished. Instead they used pure, bright colours – reds and blues, yellows, whites and greens – and put down their paint in rough brush strokes which gave the impression of light being reflected from natural surfaces.

The Impressionist method suited Vincent's purposes – like them, he liked to work fast and out-

Kröller-Müller Museum, Otterlo

a year he worked himself to breaking point, painting up to 16 hours a day. He had always worked in frenzied bursts of activity, heedless of his deteriorating health, but now he scarcely stopped to eat or drink, almost as if aware of the short lifespan allotted to him.

EXAGGERATING THE COLOUR

Every day, through the blazing heat of the summer, he would march out and set up his easel. In the autumn he tried unsuccessfully to defy the fierce southern wind, the Mistral, by pinning his canvas to the ground with heavy boulders. He would paint all night, if necessary. To give himself enough light to paint *The Café Terrace*, he stuck candles round his broad-brimmed hat and along the top of his easel, and as the bemused Arlesiens looked on, he began to paint, 'absolutely piling on, exaggerating the colour'.

Vincent had always painted with thick layers of colour. Even for some of the Dutch pictures he had applied paint so liberally that individual brushmarks were ineffective, and he resorted to squeezing paint straight from the tube on to the canvas, then modelling it 'a little' with his brush. Though he subsequently learned to texture his surfaces with great sensitivity, this thickly-applied paint – known as *impasto* – remained a hallmark of Van Gogh's art.

Musée d'Orsay, Paris/Bulloz

National Museum Vincent van Gogh, Amsterdam

Parisian street scenes
In Paris, Vincent began painting pictures of the city in the bright colours and blocky brushstrokes which were used by the Impressionists. The Restaurant de la Sirène (1887) *shows a view near Emile Bernard's studio.*

National Museum Vincent van Gogh

Van Gogh painting
(above) Bernard made this sketch of Vincent painting in Paris. The two artists had met at Fernand Cormon's studio.

Expressive colour
In this late watercolour of Stone Steps in the Hospital Garden (1889), *the blue leaves and purple tree trunk reveal Vincent's aim to 'express myself forcibly' through the use of colour.*

By 'exaggerating the colour', he explained to his brother Theo, he wished 'to express myself forcibly'. Colours for Van Gogh did not merely describe objects, but gave them meaning; and no colour meant more to him than yellow. In Japan it symbolized friendship. It represented the glory of the sun and the golden wheat – in short, it was the colour of creation. Even in his night pictures yellow plays a surprisingly important part. And in his famous painting *Sunflowers* (p.92) he created a whole painting with little colour other than yellow, a technical feat almost without parallel.

THE POWER OF YELLOW

Letters to Theo requesting paint highlight Vincent's preference. They always start with demands for large tubes of yellow and white paint. And the other colours he used heavily, especially purples and blues, serve to accentuate the power of yellow. His concern for colour extended to the framing

of each work, and it was not uncommon for him to give very explicit instructions to ensure the right effect: on one occasion he asked for a royal blue and gold frame to be designed especially for his canvas.

In the months before his breakdown, Vincent produced some 200 paintings, including about 50 portraits of his friends in Arles. Frequently he completed a painting in a single day – an amazing work-rate, even by the standards of the Impressionists. 'I was right,' he wrote to Theo, 'to work at white heat as long as it was fine.' And when his brother once hinted that his enormous output might adversely affect the quality of his work, he retorted that 'Quick work does not mean less serious work, it depends on one's self-confidence and experience.'

Under the crushing weight of mental collapse, Van Gogh's self-confidence became badly bruised. The swirling lines which distinguish all his late paintings seem to echo the torment in his mind.

COMPARISONS
Inspired by Japan

Japanese prints were popular and cheap when Van Gogh arrived in Paris in 1886. Japan had only been trading with the West for 20 years, and there was a craze for anything Japanese. Like many other artists, including Gauguin, Van Gogh was impressed and influenced by their bold designs, decorative colours and strong outlines and was a keen collector.

National Museum Vincent van Gogh, Amsterdam

Philadelphia Museum of Art: The Louis E. Stern Collection

Utagawa Hiroshige (1797-1858) **Ohashi Bridge in the Rain** *(left) Van Gogh made a copy of this wood-cut, which was one of the many Japanese prints he collected. It shows the bright colour and simplicity of design which typified Japanese art, and appealed so strongly to Van Gogh and his contemporaries.*

Paul Gauguin (1848-1903) **Self-Portrait** *(above) Gauguin painted this picture as a gift for Vincent: it combines a self-portrait with a small portrait of their mutual friend Emile Bernard. With its clear outlines, and flat decorative quality, it shows the elements which all three artists admired in Japanese art.*

Yet in this final phase of his career, Vincent still worked at a punishing pace, producing a further 200 paintings in the last year of his life. Among them was one of his greatest masterpieces – the *Self-Portrait* of 1890 (p.97). One in a series of self-portraits equalled only by Rembrandt's for their candour and penetration, it is a painting almost without colour, dominated by pale, icy colours; warmed only by the orange-brown of the artist's hair and beard.

Café Terrace at Night (1888)
(below right) Painted in Arles, this picture shows the method of using dashes of colour which Vincent had learnt in Paris. The technique is particularly obvious – and appropriate – in the cobblestones of the street. The detail (below) clearly illustrates another characteristic technique – how thickly he applied the paint. The heavy layers of yellow make the café light glow warmly against the dark blue of the night.

TRADEMARKS
Dashes and Swirls

The pictures Van Gogh painted between 1886 and 1888 use the Impressionist technique of applying the paint in dashes.

In the last two years of his life Vincent painted in waves and swirls, applied so thickly that the marks stand above the canvas.

Trevor Lawrence

Kröller-Müller Museum, Otterlo

Van Gogh on Art

I have a terrible lucidity at moments when nature is so beautiful. I am not conscious of myself any more, and the pictures come to me as if in a dream.

It is no more easy to make a good picture than it is to find a diamond or a pearl. It means trouble, and you risk your life for it.

I cannot help it that my paintings do not sell. The time will come when people will see that they are worth more than the price of the paint.

THE MAKING OF A MASTERPIECE

The Bedroom at Arles

Van Gogh painted this bedroom in his 'Yellow House' at Arles in the autumn of 1888, while awaiting Gauguin's arrival. It was one of a series of pictures he made to decorate the house and – he hoped – impress his friend. He had been living alone in Arles for months, and now he hoped the house would become the headquarters of an artists' colony, with Gauguin as its leader.

He painted the room as simply as possible, with pure, harmonious colours and strongly outlined shapes. The room is shown empty of people, but with an air of expectancy: everything is painted in pairs. The two pairs of pictures, two pillows, and especially the two chairs may well reflect Vincent's excitement that his solitude was about to end.

Vincent's Chair
(left) The bedroom chairs were part of a set of rustic furniture that Vincent bought for his proposed artists' colony. In December 1888, when he realized that Gauguin was likely to abandon him, he painted his own chair – identified by his pipe and tobacco – in isolation.

A sketch for Gauguin
(right) Vincent included this sketch in a letter which he wrote to Gauguin in September 1888, describing his painting as 'an interior of nothing at all' in which he hoped to express 'absolute restfulness'.

The National Gallery

National Museum Vincent van Gogh, Amsterdam

The Yellow House
(above) Vincent's home from the spring of 1888 stood in the Place Lamartine (right), near the river Rhône in Arles.

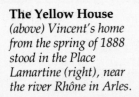

Russell Barnet

> 'A painting to rest the brain – or the imagination'   Vincent van Gogh

National Museum Vincent van Gogh, Amsterdam

Dark outlines
(above) This still-life detail shows Van Gogh's method of painting objects with flat areas of colour with bold outlines – a technique he adopted from Japanese art.

National Museum Vincent van Gogh, Amsterdam

Vincent's house
When Van Gogh lived in Arles, his Yellow House – a small two-up, two-down building on the corner of a square – was a private house attached to a food shop. Later the whole building was converted into a bar. It was bombed in 1944.

Art Institute of Chicago

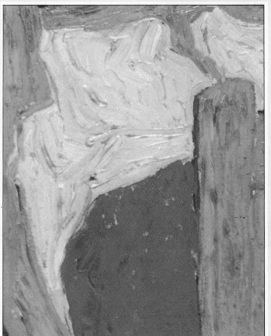

Thickly-painted pillows
Vincent nearly always loaded his brush heavily, and applied the paint thickly. In this detail, the individual brushstrokes can be seen, bounded by ridges of paint.

Gallery

Van Gogh's reputation is based on pictures painted in the last four years of his life, for his arrival in Paris in 1886 brought a complete change in his style. The bright paintings of the Impressionists and the bold designs of Japanese prints inspired him to abandon his dark pictures of peasant life and instead paint colourful canvases of his closest

Archiv für Kunst und Geschichte

Père Tanguy *1887*
25″ × 19″ Niarchos Collection, Athens

Van Gogh made several portraits of Père Tanguy, who ran an art supplies shop in Paris where penniless artists could meet and exchange their works for paint and canvases. The pictures lining the walls behind the old man are Vincent's own copies of Japanese prints.

friends and his daily environment.

Père Tanguy is among the first in a series of close-up portraits of his friends which he continued after moving to Arles, where he painted the Postman Roulin. In the brilliant southern sunshine his colours became still brighter, with yellow predominating as it does in Bedroom at Arles and Sunflowers.

Within months of painting these pictures, Van Gogh suffered a mental collapse. Cornfield and Cypresses, and Starry Night were among the 200 canvases he painted while he was in St Rémy asylum, and the troubled Church at Auvers and his late Self Portrait both seem to presage his tragic suicide.

The Postman Roulin *1888*
31¼" × 25" Museum of Fine Arts, Boston

The Postman Joseph Roulin was one of Vincent's few friends in Arles; he posed for him several times. In this portrait, the postman sits alertly, with raised eyebrows and a direct gaze. The painting has a humorous quality, accentuated by Roulin's full, fish-tail beard.

The Bedroom at Arles *1888/9*
28½″ × 36″ Art Institute of Chicago

This famous painting shows the bedroom in Van Gogh's house at Arles, which he had decorated and furnished himself. To express 'a feeling of perfect rest', he showed his room in an uncharacteristically tidy state, containing only a few objects, which he painted in pure colours with strongly-drawn outlines. However, there is something unsettling about the painting: the lines of the floor and bed seem to rush back in a disturbing way. This is one of three virtually identical versions of the painting – an indication of the importance Van Gogh attached to his room.

Sunflowers *1888*
36¼″ × 28¾″ National Gallery, London

This is one of several versions of what is probably Van Gogh's best-known painting. In 1987, one of the Sunflower paintings was sold at Christie's auction rooms, London, for £25 million to Yashuda Fire and Marine Insurance, Japan.

Cornfield and Cypresses *1889*
28⅜″ × 35¾″ National Gallery, London

After his admission to St Rémy mental asylum, Vincent was allowed out to paint – under supervision. He was fascinated by the cypress trees in the south of France, and painted them many times, often emphasising their writhing, flame-like shapes.

The Starry Night *(1889)*
29″ × 36¼″ Collection, The Museum of Modern Art,
New York

One of several 'starry night' pictures which Van Gogh painted, this version shows virtually the same view as Cornfield and Cypresses *(p.93), but under a night sky. The light from the larger-than-life stars and crescent moon is shown by haloes of yellow and white paint: these expanding circles, built up of dashes of colour, are often seen in Van Gogh's later works.*

The Church at Auvers *1890*
37″ × 29″ Musée d'Orsay, Paris

Vincent moved to Auvers in northern France after he left the St Rémy asylum. This picture of the village church – with its strange perspective, twisted shapes, and harsh colour – was painted the month before he committed suicide.

Self-Portrait *1890*
25⅝″ × 17¾″ Musée d'Orsay, Paris

In one of his last self-portraits, Vincent shows himself tense and tired after a series of breakdowns. His jacket merges with the pale swirling background, while his red beard stands out strongly.

The Impressionists in Paris

When Van Gogh visited Paris in 1874, the Impressionists had just shocked the art world with their first exhibition. He returned 10 years later to form a 'second wave', with Gauguin and Lautrec.

Edouard Manet
The 'Father of Impressionism', Manet was a fashionable man-about-town – a most unlikely revolutionary.

The Mansell Collection

Manet's outrageous painting
The Luncheon on the Grass (1863) *broke art's most sacred convention: nudes should be goddesses, not real women sitting with fully-dressed gentlemen.*

Vincent van Gogh first visited Paris at the age of 21, when he stayed with his brother Theo. Obsessed by the failure of a love affair, he spent much of his free time sitting indoors, brooding over the Bible. Vincent had not yet decided to become a painter, and – though both he and Theo worked for a firm of art dealers – he was scarcely aware that a revolution in painting was fomenting in the city.

In April 1874, just before he arrived, a group of painters known as the Impressionists had held their first exhibition at a shop owned by the photographer Nadar, in the Boulevard des Capucines. A mixed band of individualists, they included the buoyant, self-confident Claude Monet and the day-dreaming Auguste Renoir, the anarchist Camille Pissarro and the elegant Edgar Degas.

The group had come together in 1863, when their father figure, Edouard Manet, outraged the Paris art world with his *Luncheon on the Grass* – a painting of a naked woman picnicking with two fully-clothed men. The subject was an affront to bourgeois taste, and it was turned down by the selection panel of the Académie des Beaux Arts as unsuitable for showing at the annual exhibition of the Salon.

In previous years such a picture would never have reached the public eye. But that same year, the Emperor Napoleon III had given a new opportunity to rejected artists by opening a second exhibition, the Salon des Refusés, especially for

Claude Monet
The son of a grocer in Le Havre, Monet became the central figure of Impressionism – and a regular visitor to Manet's favourite haunt, the Café Guerbois. The closeness of the two artists' names often caused confusion. Manet was once furious to read a good review of Monet's work, believing the critic to have mistaken his identity.

Renoir/Portrait of Monet/Musée Marmottan

Roger Viollet

Camille Pissarro
The oldest of the Impressionists, Pissarro joined the 'gang' at the Café Guerbois. He encouraged many younger artists, including Van Gogh, Gauguin and Cézanne – who once described him as 'humble and colossal, something like God the Father.'

Bulloz

Musée d'Orsay, Paris

Pissarro/Self-Portrait

them. Over 1,000 painters showed their works, and Manet's *Luncheon* caused a sensation. The academic critics savaged the painting as 'a shameful, open sore,' but Manet quickly became a hero for the young radicals. They flocked to his studio for advice and encouragement. And their sense of common purpose was cemented by meetings in the nearby Café Guerbois.

NIGHTS IN THE CAFE GUERBOIS

Every Thursday, as the light faded in the evening, the painters would meet up to discuss their ideas with other leaders of the avant garde – novelists such as Emile Zola and poets such as Charles Baudelaire and Théophile Gautier. Over numerous glasses of wine or absinthe, the popular but lethal anis-flavoured drink of the time, they would engage in fierce debate about their artistic aims. Sometimes the arguments would get out of hand – Manet himself was once almost provoked into fighting a duel there.

For all but a few of the younger artists, there were two overriding goals – to paint the everyday world around them, and to work in the open air. It was Monet who was initially most interested in painting landscapes. Others soon followed his example, for working in the countryside was cheap, and it was stimulating to have company. The Impressionists would often work together at Bougival and Argenteuil on the Seine, in the Forest of Fontainebleau, or on the coast of Normandy.

While the artists spent much of their time in these tranquil settings, they would regularly travel to Paris to try to sell some paintings. They found it hard to make a living. Not only was their work still barred from the official Salon, where professional artists could attract commissions, but the expensive galleries of the 'grands boulevards' also refused to stock their paintings. Buyers were hard to find, even with prices as low as 20 to 40 francs.

The Impressionists were not without minor patrons, such as Pissarro's friends Murer the confectioner and Dr de Bellio; the singer Fauré who collected Manet; the civil servant Chocquet who supported Renoir and Cézanne; or the anarchist Père Tanguy, a supplier of art materials who gave them all generous credit as well as paint and canvas in return for their paintings.

But it was against a background of penury, obscurity and growing frustration that the artists had conceived the idea of a group exhibition, in an attempt to bring their work directly to the attention of the buying public. Only Manet refused to exhibit with them: he was exhausted by the ten-

The cafés of Paris
Manet's painting The Waitress (1878) *shows an artist in his blue smock drinking at a café. The Impressionists met weekly in such places to debate their work.*

The photographer Nadar
Gaspard Félix Tournachon, known as Nadar, was a photographer and balloonist. This portrait was taken at his studio in Boulevard des Capucines, which he lent to the Impressionists for their first exhibition in 1874.

The National Gallery

The Mansell Collection

National Museum Vincent van Gogh, Amsterdam

The picture trade
(below) A Montmartre junk-shop offering paintings for sale gives a vivid glimpse of the art trade in the back streets, or 'petits boulevards.' One famous dealer, Père Tanguy, ran a similar store selling art supplies and built up a huge collection of unsaleable pictures, which he took in exchange for paint and canvases. Tanguy's shop was a haven for the Impressionists from Cézanne to Van Gogh, who painted the dealer's portrait on several occasions.

Mary Evans Picture Library

Van Gogh at Le Tambourin
Toulouse-Lautrec painted this portrait of his friend in their favourite café, Le Tambourin in Montmartre. Gauguin described the place as 'a real cut-throat's den', but it had much to recommend it: cheap drink, a lively cabaret and a colourful, if argumentative, clientele.

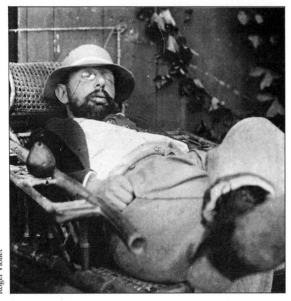

Roger Viollet

Women of Montmartre
Many of the cafés in Montmartre were shabby and run-down places where no respectable lady would be seen. The women who frequented them were generally prostitutes, who often modelled for artists.

Toulouse-Lautrec
(left) Lautrec met Van Gogh and Gauguin in Paris during the mid-1880s, when the first Impressionist circle was beginning to break up. The new generation of artists were known as Post-Impressionists.

year barrage of criticisms and personal abuse, and no longer wished to expose his work to ridicule.

The first exhibition, which took place just before Vincent arrived in Paris, proved a financial failure, and was predictably slammed by the critics as indecent 'filth'. But it represented the first stage in an outbreak of artistic defiance which would soon transform the French art world. When Vincent arrived back in Paris in 1886, the Impressionists were on their way to commercial success.

Eight exhibitions in 12 years had generated a growing momentum of critical approval. Renoir had even won approval from the academic establishment, with a painting prominently displayed at the 1879 Salon, after which Pissarro wrote, 'I do believe Renoir is launched. So much the better! It's so hard to be poor.' And if the other Impressionists were still not entirely accepted by the art-buying clientele, their paintings were now selling in reasonable quantities through more progressive dealers such as Durand-Ruel who, in 1886, staged a most successful exhibition in New York.

Theo van Gogh himself stocked works by Monet, Degas, Renoir and Pissarro in his Montmartre gallery and the two brothers would often discuss the new developments. Vincent was now committed to a painting career, and in a much more receptive frame of mind altogether. He quickly realized that the Impressionist painters were a force to be reckoned with.

VAN GOGH MEETS PISSARRO

Shortly after Vincent's arrival, Theo introduced his brother to Pissarro, who was known for being sensitive and encouraging to young artists. Vincent had great respect for Pissarro's judgement. On one occasion, dressed in his characteristic blue workman's smock, he stopped his mentor in a busy street and insisted on showing him his latest canvases, in full view of mocking passers-by. Pissarro said later he felt Vincent would either 'go mad or leave the Impressionists far behind', not realizing that both of these predictions would be entirely fulfilled.

In fact, Impressionism had already passed its peak as a dynamic movement. The leaders had argued with each other, and begun to go in different directions. With no progressive schools available, Vincent was forced to enrol at an 'official' studio, run by Fernand Cormon, a man who detested Impressionism. There he made friends with other students including Emile Bernard and Louis Anquetin, the Australian John Russell and an engaging, rather ugly aristocrat, Henri de Toulouse-Lautrec. This group, with Paul Gauguin and Georges Seurat, would soon form a new wave in the Paris art world.

After a few months, Vincent and Toulouse-Lautrec left the Cormon studio in frustration. They had already met other more stimulating painters at Père Tanguy's art supplies shop in the back streets of Montmartre. The generous Tanguy, who still

The hills of Montmartre
In the 1880s Montmartre was still a village on the northern edge of Paris, dotted with picturesque windmills and crowned by the church of Sacré Coeur. Exempt from the Paris alcohol tax, it became a centre for night-clubs and entertainment and a popular home for artists.

displayed Impressionist works in his shop, one day introduced Vincent to Cézanne, who also had a reputation for being furiously emotional. It was not an encouraging meeting. After studying Vincent's recent work, Cézanne said bluntly, 'You certainly paint like a madman.'

The volatile circle of artists around Van Gogh styled themselves as the 'groupe du petit boulevard', in ironic contrast to the Impressionists who had now made their way into the galleries of the 'grands boulevards.' Their output was feverishly prolific, the subjects for paintings often being drawn from the picturesque Montmartre environment with its windmills and quiet lanes.

Like the Impressionists before them, these 'Post-Impressionists' spent long hours in cafés arguing over glasses of absinthe – particularly Vincent, his outspoken friend Gauguin and the urbane Toulouse-Lautrec. One of their favourite haunts was the tavern Le Tambourin on the Boulevard de Clichy, described by Gauguin as 'a real cut-throat's den.' Its owner, Agostina Segatori, even agreed to display some of her clients' paintings.

But while the artists harangued each other in the Café Tambourin – till on one occasion an exasperated customer hit Vincent over the head with a still life – they found it very difficult to get exhibited. Without sales, the group could not survive in the expensive capital. Soon Gauguin and Bernard left Paris for Brittany, and in 1888 Van Gogh took the train to Arles. It would take almost a decade for Paris to discover its loss.

A Year in the Life 1888

While Van Gogh was furnishing his Yellow House in Arles, France was shaken by political strife. In Paris, the ex-War Minister General Boulanger was wounded in a duel with Prime Minister Flocquet, while Kaiser Wilhelm of Germany made ominous threats of war. In Britain, Jack the Ripper stalked the streets of London – and heavy snow fell in mid-summer.

Dunlop's new invention

The pneumatic tyre was introduced in 1888 by John Boyd Dunlop, a Belfast vet. This, combined with the improved safety bicycle, suddenly made bicycling a very popular pastime – not least because it brought a change in fashion and women could show their legs.

Lauros-Giraudon

Jean Beraud/Cyclists in the Bois de Boulogne/©DACS 1988

Mary Evans Picture Library

Eiffel tower in progress

Alexandre Gustave Eiffel was a French engineer whose name was made famous by the tower he designed for the Paris Exhibition of 1889. This tower was a feat of 19th century engineering which revealed the potential of steel construction and stands today as one of the wonders of the modern world.

An American astrologer predicted that this year would see the world's last days, with the sun turning to blood and 'one universal carnage of death'. It started badly: in January and February, deep snow and ferocious frosts brought most of Europe to a standstill. The French astronomer Camille Flammarion, a recognized authority on the end of the world, warned that the cold spell defied normal explanation. In Birmingham, word went round that the Day of Judgement had arrived. And in London, Edward Maitland wrote that the world had ended and another was being born.

This was right in one sense. The comforting edifice of nineteenth-century science had begun to crumble. Michelson and Morley, experimenting in Berlin on the speed of light, were destroying the idea of a fixed universe and paving the way for Einstein's theory of relativity. In Vienna Ernst Mach, whose excellent work on the speed of sound would give a new word to the language, insisted that it was no longer possible to believe in absolute space or absolute time.

FICTION TRUER THAN FACT

Men of imagination, artists and writers, stepped into the breach, claiming their insights were more valuable than those of the scientists. Fiction, declared Robert Louis Stevenson, was closer to truth than 'the dazzle and confusion of reality'. The German philosopher Friedrich Nietzsche summed the matter up more pithily: 'The old God has abdicated, and from now on I shall rule the world.'

The Illustrated London News

Mary Evans Picture Library

Boulanger's Duel
In 1888, General Boulanger insulted Floquet, Prime Minister of France, who responded with a challenge. Boulanger had choice of weapons and chose swords. Being a soldier, 10 years younger than his opponent, it looked as though odds were on his side. But he was badly wounded in the throat: Floquet was the victor. The British press were scathing about the duel, as duelling had been outlawed in England about 20 years beforehand.

Mary Evans Picture Library

Fridtjof Nansen
Nansen's imagination was fired by his first sight of Greenland's mighty ice cap, and he determined to cross it. His expedition of six left Norway in May 1888. After enduring intense cold they reached the summit in September. Nansen was also a scientist and, later, a statesman, winning the Nobel peace prize in 1922 for work with refugees.

Jack the Ripper
Jack the Ripper was the name given to the unknown murderer of seven prostitutes, late in 1888. His nickname came from the terrible multilation of their bodies.

Like Van Gogh, Nietzsche felt threatened by approaching insanity. Yet there was much to suggest the world around them was at least as mad as they were. When Van Gogh arrived in Arles early in 1888 he found a city torn by violence and by wild racial hatreds. Italian workmen were attacked by angry crowds and half-strangled before local contractors were finally persuaded to stop employing them. Throughout France, people became impatient with their dull Republican government, and looked for something less rational, more flamboyant. General Boulanger, until recently Minister for War, seemed ready to take over.

On 15 March, the day after the troubles in Arles had come to a head, Boulanger was stripped of his army commission. Forbidden to go to Paris because of his suspected intrigues against the Republic, he had dared to go there in disguise, 'wearing dark spectacles and affecting lameness'. The attempt to disgrace him only made him more popular and he was elected to the Chamber of Deputies by two separate constituencies – for one of which he had not even been a candidate.

BOULANGER'S DUEL

Boulanger then tried to sweep away the Republic by getting the Chamber to dissolve itself and challenged the Prime Minister, Charles Floquet, to a duel. When the duel was fought Boulanger 'with blind impetuosity spitted himself on Monsieur Floquet's sword', receiving a severe wound in the throat, while Floquet sustained only minor injuries. Three days later a group

The Football League

The Football League was formed in 1888 to stimulate interest in soccer. There were 12 founder clubs, including Everton and Aston Villa – still amongst the strongest in England.

Tesla's electrical machine

The Croatian scientist Nikola Tesla developed alternating current machinery in America, competing with Edison's direct current system. In 1888 he was conducting experiments which three years later led to the Tesla coil – still used today in radios and televisions.

The rise of lawn tennis

Lawn tennis – a development of real, or 'royal' tennis – was first played in the 1870s and within a decade was so popular throughout the Western world that numerous national associations were formed: among them the U.S. Lawn Tennis Association in 1881 and the British Lawn Tennis Association in 1888.

Mary Evans Picture Library

of shocked and peaceable deputies tried to get duelling banned, but were overwhelmingly defeated. Boulanger's popularity continued to grow.

Colourful swashbucklers, however impetuous, were more to French taste than the frock-coated politicians of the Republic. This was partly because the Republic no longer seemed respectable. A deputy called Daniel Wilson, who had married the President's daughter, had used his position to further his own interest as a newspaper proprietor. There were other scandals in the offing, as politicians became more and more enmeshed in the shady dealings of the company which had been formed to build the Panama Canal.

Paris was hit by a wave of strikes, as well as other forms of violence: anarchists and communists waged an open gun battle

in Père Lachaise cemetery and an artist, Eugène Dupuis, was killed by another artist in a duel about their paintings. The bloodletting fell a long way short of the universal carnage forecast by astrologers, but continued to undermine the solid values of the Republic.

THE BELLIGERENT KAISER

One man who did talk about carnage was the new German Emperor, Wilhelm II, who came to the throne in June. Within a week of his accession he had two French newspaper correspondents thrown out of Berlin, and embarked on a series of official visits to countries that might be Germany's allies in any future war with France.

Rudyard Kipling

1888 saw the publication of Kipling's first major work – Plain Tales from the Hills, *set in India, where he lived as a child and worked as a young man. Within a year Kipling had made his reputation as one of the most brilliant prose writers of the time. Today he is best known for his children's stories and his championing of British imperialism.*

Mary Evans Picture Library

Josef F. Martin-Artothek

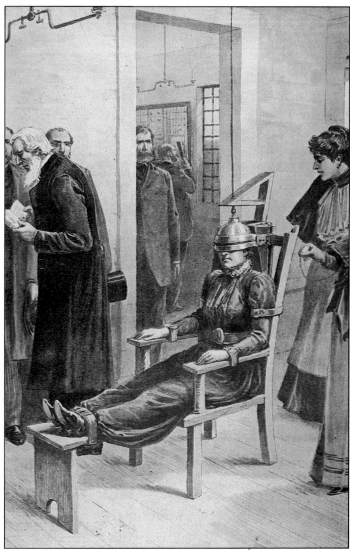

Mary Evans Picture Library

The electric chair

Electrocution was adopted as a form of capital punishment in 1888 in New York; it is supposed to be painless. After sedation, the prisoner is strapped into an electric chair in the death chamber. Metal plates are attached to the head and legs and a current of 2200 volts passes through the prisoner's body resulting in almost immediate death.

John Lavery/The Tennis Party/Aberdeen Art Gallery

In August, the Kaiser made an uncompromising speech, saying that if France tried to recover the German provinces of Alsace and Lorraine, more than 40 million Germans would rather 'be left dead on the battlefield than see one stone taken from them'. A few weeks later the imperial coat of arms above the German consulate in Le Havre was torn down. The French government made hasty apologies, but the Boulangists exulted.

Italy, fearing a French attack on La Spezia, allied herself with Germany but Britain stood aloof, untroubled by these continental squabbles. Instead she turned to such dull matters as the establishment of County Councils and floating a new issue of government stock.

Britain's own favourite prophet, the medieval wise woman known as Mother Shipton, had said the world would come to an end when summer turned into winter; this happened in 1888, with snow in June and July, but the British remained unperturbed. Yet they did see their own brand of sadistic violence, with Jack the Ripper's murders in the East End of London.

As the tension mounted, and Boulanger won election after election in an atmosphere charged with anti-German delirium, his advent to power seemed inevitable. But January 1889 saw a farcical anti-climax. Cheering crowds in Paris tried to install him in the Presidential Palace, but Boulanger refused to budge. His opportunity passed and the French Republic was saved, along with the peace of Europe. The end of the old world, the predicted 'universal carnage of death', was put off for 25 years, until the terrible days of August 1914.

The Times attacks Parnell

The Irish leader Charles Parnell gained many enemies for his Home Rule policy. In 1887 The Times published a forged letter, supposedly from Parnell condoning the murders of the Chief Secretary of Ireland and his undersecretary. The furore continued through 1888 until the following year when the forger was caught and confessed under interrogation – and Parnell became a hero overnight.

Mary Evans Picture Library

De Beers Consolidated Mines

The Bridgeman Art Library

Kaiser Wilhelm II

Wilhelm became Emperor in 1888 at the age of 29 and modelled himself on the Prussian ideal of the tough warrior king. On the eve of World War I he supported his generals' grandiose war aims, ruling out all chance of peace. Forced to abdicate in 1918 after Germany lost the war, he spent the rest of his life in exile in the Netherlands.

Diamond mines in South Africa

In 1888 the diamond mines of Kimberley finally came under the control of Cecil Rhodes and the firm of De Beers Consolidated Mines Ltd was established.

A. Strassberger/William II

Ernest Laurent: Seurat at 23/Musée d'Art Moderne, Paris

1859-1891

Georges Seurat is best known for his novel technique of painting in tiny dots of colour – the method known as 'Pointillism', which he devised according to rigid scientific principles. A proud man, but extremely shy by nature, he spent most of his time reading books or painting in the isolation of his studio. He was intensely secretive, jealously guarding his latest discoveries from even his closest friends.

Seurat was attracted by much the same subjects as his Impressionist contemporaries – seascapes, summer by the River Seine, the entertainers of the Parisian night-clubs. But instead of recording fleeting impressions, he imposed a sense of stillness and order on his world. Seurat's whole career was compressed into 12 years of patient activity. He died tragically young, probably from meningitis, at the age of 31.

The Quiet Experimenter

A man of independent means, Seurat devoted his short life entirely to art. He worked alone, and was so secretive that even his close friends were unaware that he had a wife and son.

Georges-Pierre Seurat was born in Paris on 2 December 1859, the son of comfortably-off parents. His father, a legal official, was a solitary man with a taciturn and withdrawn manner which his son also inherited. At every available opportunity, Antoine-Chrisostôme took leave of his family and disappeared to his villa in the suburbs to grow flowers and say mass in the company of his gardener; he was only at home on Tuesdays. Seurat's mother was quiet and unassuming, but it was she who gave some warmth and continuity to his childhood.

Hidden depths
Seurat's personality was reserved but strong. A contemporary wrote of him: 'Imagine a tall young man, extremely shy, yet of great physical energy . . . . He is one of those peaceable yet stubborn men who may appear afraid of everything, but who actually do not flinch at any challenge.'

The family apartment was on the Boulevard de Magenta, close to the landscaped pleasure garden the Parc des Buttes-Chaumont, where young Georges and his mother spent much of their spare time. Such places, and the people who frequented them, were to become the subject of some of his greatest paintings.

THE HANDSOME STUDENT

As a young man, Seurat was tall and handsome with 'velvety eyes' and a quiet, gentle voice. Reserved and dignified in dress as well as manner, he was always neatly and correctly turned out: one friend described him as looking like a floor-walker in a department store, while the sophisticated and sharp-tongued Edgar Degas nicknamed him 'the notary'. He was serious and intense – preferring to spend his money on books rather than on food or drink – but his most pronounced characteristic was his secretiveness.

Despite many of the qualities of the perfect student, Seurat did not particularly shine at school or at the Ecole des Beaux-Arts, the official Paris art school, which he entered in 1878. But thanks to a regular allowance, he never had any need to sell his work for a living – nor to produce work that was saleable. In 1879, a year of military service

La Grande Jatte
In Seurat's day the island of La Grande Jatte – in the River Seine, on the outskirts of Paris – was a popular weekend pleasure resort. Seurat visited the island frequently, and chose it as the setting for his largest painting.

Bernard Regent/Camerapix Hutchison Agency

Seurat's champion

(below) The writer Félix Fénéon vigorously defended Seurat and his avant-garde friends at a time when they were subjected to much critical abuse. This extraordinary portrait of Fénéon was painted in 1890 by Paul Signac. It shows him sporting his distinctive 'Uncle Sam' beard.

Friend and disciple

(right) Paul Signac was a valuable friend who introduced Seurat to other artists. An accomplished painter himself, he also wrote a book explaining Seurat's scientific theories of painting, and adopted many of his friend's ideas. Seurat drew this portrait in about 1889.

Edimages

David Rockefeller Collection, New York

broke into his artistic studies. Seurat was sent to the great military port of Brest on the western coast of Brittany, where he fitted in easily to barracks discipline and used his spare time to begin sketching figures and ships.

Returning to Paris in 1880, the young artist initially shared a cramped studio on the Left Bank with two student friends before moving to a studio of his own, closer to his parents' home on the Right Bank. For the next two years, he devoted himself to mastering the art of black and white drawing.

The year 1883 was spent working on a huge canvas, *Bathing at Asnières* (pp.118-19), his first major painting. In 1884, the Salon jury rejected it and Seurat changed the direction of his career. From this year on, he scorned the academic art of the Salon and allied himself with the young independent painters.

An instinctively gifted painter, Seurat also had extraordinary powers of concentration and perseverance, and took a dogged and single-minded approach to work. He was convinced of the rightness of his own opinions, and of the importance of the 'pointillist' method he was

developing. Although other painters turned to him as a leader, he seems to have inspired admiration rather than affection. He in turn looked upon this admiration as naturally befitting his superior intellect, hard work and achievement.

MEMBER OF THE COMMITTEE

In May and June 1884, Seurat's *Bathing at Asnières* hung at the first exhibition of the new group of Artistes Indépendants, mounted in a temporary hut near the ruined Tuileries Palace. The show ended in financial muddle, but out of the ensuing arguments a properly constituted Société des Artistes Indépendants emerged, committed to holding an annual show with no jury. Seurat attended its committee meetings regularly, always sitting in the same seat, quietly smoking his pipe.

At one such meeting, Seurat struck up a friendship with Paul Signac. Signac was four years younger, a largely self-taught painter who was influenced by the Impressionists and very receptive to Seurat's theoretical ideas. The extrovert and enthusiastic Signac provided Seurat

J. Toorop/The Three Brides/Kröller-Müller Museum, Otterlo

©DACS 1988

A Belgian friend
*Theo van Rysselberghe –
here caricatured by himself
– was a Belgian artist who
admired Seurat's work.*

with contacts and moral support as he set about making his mark within the avant-garde.

In the summer of 1884, Seurat embarked on another major canvas, again depicting the popular boating place of Asnières, but this time focusing on the island of La Grande Jatte in the Seine. With characteristic single-mindedness, he devoted his time entirely to the composition. Every day for months he travelled to his chosen spot, where he would work all morning. Each afternoon, he continued painting the giant canvas in his studio.

After two years of concentrated, systematic work, Seurat completed the painting in 1886, and exhibited it with the Impressionist group in May of that year. *La Grand Jatte* (p.122-3) proved to be the main talking point of the exhibition, and he was hailed by the critics as offering the most significant way forward from Impressionism. Félix Fénéon, a sensitive and sympathetic young critic, was particularly impressed. He christened Seurat and his associates the Neo-Impressionists, and became an enthusiastic spokesman for them. In a series of articles on contemporary art in the newly-launched *Vogue* magazine, Fénéon paid special attention to Seurat's work, and expounded his new method in scientific detail.

CENTRE OF CONTROVERSY

Suddenly, Seurat found that he was the most controversial figure on the artistic scene in Paris. He was now occupying a studio next to Signac's on the Boulevard de Clichy in Montmartre. Here he was surrounded by artists ranging from the conservative decorator Puvis de Chavannes, whom he greatly admired, to more progressive contemporaries – including Degas, Gauguin, Van Gogh and Toulouse-Lautrec. He was at the centre

A fashion for decadence
Through Signac, Seurat came into contact with many contemporary artists, including the Dutchman Jan Toorop, who painted The Three Brides (1893), *a famous example of the fashionable taste for 'decadence'. Like Toorop, Seurat exhibited with the avant-garde Belgian group Les Vingt (The Twenty) – and in fact Seurat was better received in Brussels than in Paris.*

Summers in Honfleur
(right) Seurat often spent the summer at this port, and other resorts on the Normandy coast. Seascapes and harbour views formed a major part of his output as a painter.

of artistic debates, but he kept aloof from them.

Seurat's relative financial ease meant that he was unused to dealing with potential clients, and his demands remained modest despite his new fame. Once, when pressed to name his price for the painting he was showing at 'The Twenty' exhibition in Brussels, Seurat replied, 'I compute my expenses on the basis of one year at seven francs a day'. His attitude to his work was similarly down-to-earth and unromantic – he had no pretensions to the status of genius. When some critics tried to describe his work as poetic he contradicted them: 'No, I apply my method and that is all.' He was, however, very concerned not to lose any credit for the originality of his technique and guarded the details obsessively.

Seurat's life had begun to assume a regular pattern. During the winter months, he would lock himself away in his studio working on a big figure picture to exhibit in the spring, then he would spend the summer months in one of the Normandy ports such as Honfleur, working on smaller, less complex, marine paintings. Whether in Paris or at the coast, Seurat was never a great socializer and in the last year of his life he virtually cut himself off from friends. He could warm up in a one-to-one situation, but by all accounts his conversation centred on his own artistic concerns.

A SECRET FAMILY

Late in 1889, when Seurat was approaching 30, he moved away from the bustling Boulevard de Clichy to a studio in a quieter street nearby, where – unbeknown to his family and friends – he lived with a young model, Madeleine Knobloch. In February 1890 she gave birth, in the studio, to his son. Seurat legally acknowledged the child and gave him his own Christian names in reverse. But it was not until two days before his death that he introduced his young family to his mother.

Georges Seurat died in March 1891, totally unexpectedly: he seems to have contracted a form of meningitis. One week he was helping to hang the paintings at the Indépendants exhibition and worrying about the fact that his hero Puvis de Chavannes had walked past *The Circus* (p.129) without so much as a glance; the following week he was dead. Signac sadly concluded 'our poor friend killed himself by overwork'.

Wife and Heiress

Seurat was so secretive that few people knew he had a common-law wife named Madeleine Knobloch, and after his early death even his close friends were surprised to learn that he also had a son. Seurat's parents allotted her a half-share of the paintings he left behind in his studio, but Madeleine was not content with this. She claimed that Seurat's friends were trying to 'despoil' her of his works, and these repeated accusations eventually turned everyone against her.

Seurat's tomb
(below) Seurat is buried in an imposing family vault – the third from the left – in Père Lachaise Cemetery in Paris.

Woman Powdering Herself (1890)
Seurat's wife Madeleine – model for this painting – was described as 'a poor scatterbrain'.

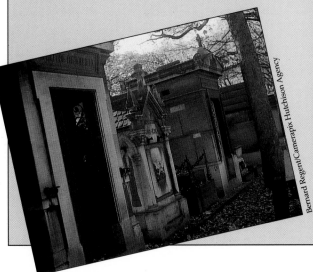

Bernard Regent/Camerapix Hutchison Agency

Courtauld Institute Galleries, London

A Pattern of Dots

With the aid of scientific treatises on colour – and his own acute powers of observation – Seurat developed a highly original technique of painting, using tiny multicoloured dots.

Seurat is best known today as the artist who devised a painstaking method of painting in tiny dots. His works as a whole, paintings and drawings alike, are characterized by their precise and deliberate quality. He left nothing to chance, never starting a picture unless he knew exactly where he was going. As one friend remarked later, 'the sensation of being carried away meant nothing to him'.

Every day, Seurat shut himself in his little studio, surrounded by his books. There he could be found perched on a step-ladder in front of one of his canvases – some of them up to ten feet long – working in silence, his eyes half closed, a little wooden pipe held tightly between his teeth. He often worked late into the night, undeterred by the poor artificial light. When he wanted a breath of air he went for long walks around Paris.

A MYRIAD OF DOTS

To begin with, he covered the canvas with a layer of paint. Over this, he painted a layer of local colours in broad textured strokes. Then he began to build up the painting using multi-coloured dots, taking small sections of the canvas at a time and working with incredible concentration. And because he had mapped out every detail in advance, he rarely needed to step back from the canvas to see the whole effect.

The Stone Breaker (c.1883)
Seurat's earliest subjects were peasants at work, toiling in the fields or at the roadside. They were painted on small wooden panels in a bold Impressionist style.

When friends came to visit Seurat, they found him reserved and uncommunicative. He only became animated when they touched upon his ideas or theories. Then he would climb down from his ladder and, taking up a piece of chalk, eagerly draw diagrams on the studio floor.

Seurat did not invent these theories. Rather he studied the aesthetic and scientific treatises of the day with a view to finding logical explanations for the colouristic qualities he had already admired in paintings. One of the key notions Seurat took up was the idea of 'optical mixture'. Instead of mixing his colours on the palette before placing them on

The Models (1888)
(below) In this 'small version', three models pose in front of Seurat's huge canvas La Grande Jatte. *Seurat probably wanted to prove that his vibrant 'dot' technique could be applied with equal effect to a studio interior or a sunny outdoor scene.*

Bridgeman Art Library

A master draughtsman
(left) Early in his career, Seurat devoted two years to mastering the art of drawing in black and white. At the 'Concert Européen' (1887-8) shows the beautiful subtlety of his technique.

The Eiffel Tower
(1889)
Seurat painted the Eiffel Tower a year before it was opened to the public, when it was highly unfashionable to like it. At that time, the tower was covered in enamel paint in various colours, so that Seurat's colourful technique was strangely suited to it.

the canvas, which made them lose their brilliance, he tried placing separate dabs of unmixed colour side by side on the canvas. He believed that they would then merge in the eye of the spectator, without any loss of vibrancy. The Impressionists had worked like this instinctively, but Seurat was able to justify the practice in logical terms.

Seurat first experimented with this novel technique in a seascape of 1885, painting in regular dots or dashes to capture more subtle changes in light effects. It was this technique that was dubbed 'pointillism'. The actual colours of the dots depended on a number of considerations: the natural colour of the scene before him, the effect of sunlight or shadow, and the reaction of one colour to another. By a logical extension of his desire to control the viewer's response, Seurat began, in 1887, to give his works painted borders.

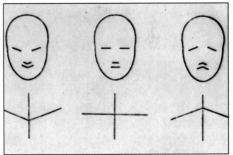

Lines of emotion
(above) Having evolved his own theory of colour, Seurat began to ponder the significance of line. From aesthetic treatises, he learned that the directions of lines could express different emotions: upward-slanting lines are happy, horizontal lines are calm and downward-sloping lines are sad.

The theory in practice
In a working sketch for his final painting, The Circus (p.129), Seurat has blocked in the main lines of the composition in blue. The lady bare-back rider sets the emotional tone of the picture – she is sketched in 'happy' lines, leaping upwards.

113

The Coast of Normandy

Many French artists painted views of the Normandy coastline, attracted by the bustling harbours, the majestic chalk cliffs, the fishing-craft and the many moods of the sea.

But each painter catches a different mood. Seurat himself liked to evoke the 'feeling the sea inspires on calm days'. Pissarro was more interested in the appearance of the ocean under different weather conditions. And Courbet responded most strongly to the rugged character of the cliffs along the seashore.

Réunion des Musées Nationaux

Louvre, Paris

Bridgeman Art Library

Tate Gallery, London

Gustave Courbet (1819-77) The Cliffs at Etretat
(above) Courbet's vigorous seascape shows a gusty day at Etretat – famous for its natural rock arch, formed by the relentless beating of wind and sea.

Camille Pissarro (1830-1903) The Pilot's Jetty, Le Havre
Pissarro gave this busy harbour scene the detailed subtitle 'Morning, grey weather, misty'. The bleak, overcast sky is reflected in the greyish green sea.

The pointillist nude
(below) Seurat's Study for The Models *(1887), shows how successfully his technique could be applied to painting a nude. The regular dots are used to convey the roundness of the model's simplified form.*

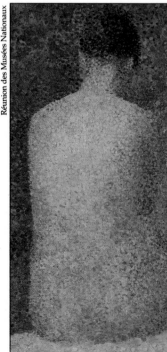

Réunion des Musées Nationaux

Musée d'Orsay, Paris

What Seurat hoped to achieve through the pointillist technique was not just greater accuracy, but also the vibration of light itself. He was hampered, unfortunately, by faulty materials. By the 1890s, his artist friend Paul Signac could already see serious discolouration and darkening in some of the colours Seurat had used.

HAPPY AND SAD LINES

From 1887 onwards, Seurat turned his restless intelligence to the problem of line. He was intrigued by contemporary theories on the directions of lines and the belief that in a painting lines could be used to convey different emotions. Upward-tending lines were thought to express gaiety, horizontal lines serenity, and downward lines sadness. He applied these theories in some of his later works, especially those depicting the artificially high-spirited world of the circus.

For his subject matter, Seurat turned his analytical eye on the contemporary world. At first he deliberately set out to explore Impressionist subjects – suburban scenes, summer landscapes and seascapes. But unlike the Impressionists,

who had tried to capture the passing moment, Seurat was fascinated by the eternal moment – the timeless grandeur of everyday life. Later he favoured themes in which people were performing: circus parades, cancan dancers, singers and clowns. In his early drawings Seurat had made studies of individual figures, which he re-used in his later compositions, but they remain isolated. Even his crowds are strangely silent.

Seurat's drawings form an important part of his output – described by Signac as 'the most beautiful painter's drawings that ever existed'. As in his paintings, Seurat organized and simplified his subject-matter to convey a fixed and lasting image. He patiently built up tones in small criss-cross strokes, using velvety conté crayon on heavy, rough-textured paper. Often he would isolate a dark silhouetted figure against a lighter background, or capture the fall of lamplight on the softened features of a face.

If Seurat can be criticised for a certain dryness and impersonality, he was nevertheless one of the most acute observers of contemporary life. The perfect balance of harmony and luminosity he achieved has never been equalled.

Painting in Dots

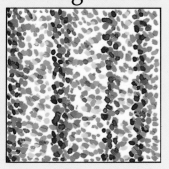

Seurat's paintings are made up of thousands of tiny, coloured dots, in which the natural colours of objects mingle with contrasting colours – red with green, orange with blue. This is known as pointillism.

Port-en-Bessin (1888) *(above and left) In this carefully composed painting of the quay at Port-en-Bessin, Seurat makes meticulous use of his pointillist technique. The dots vibrate on the canvas, suggesting the harshness of the midday sun. Stiff little figures cast short shadows, made up of red, blue and orange dots. The detail of the pavilion in the background shows just how many colours Seurat used. From a distance, these dots blend together in the eye of the onlooker.*

115

Michael McGuinness

La Grande Jatte

Seurat began work on *La Grand Jatte* (pp.122-3) in 1884, and spent nearly two years on the immense canvas. For months on end he visited the little island on the Seine, making studies of the Sunday strollers and the sunny landscape. He worked with complete concentration, moulding the real scene into the picture of his imagination – when the grass grew too long at the river's edge, he even asked his friends to cut it. Eventually Seurat began to build up the final picture in his studio, skilfully distributing his calm, static figures across the canvas. The finished work was exhibited in 1886 at the last Impressionist exhibition, where it provoked an outcry. Seurat's admirers hailed him the 'Messiah of a new art'.

Bridgeman Art Library

The emerging picture
(above) Seurat set up the ten-foot canvas in his small studio in the Boulevard de Clichy. Working from a step-ladder he painted over a speckled base, and patiently built up small areas of the picture at a time. The blobs of colour on his palette were laid out in the exact order of the spectrum.

Oil studies
(right) Seurat's loosely painted oil sketches, made on the spot, record the slow development of the picture.

Bridgeman Art Library

'La Grande Jatte unrolls before you like some myriad-speckled tapestry.'

Félix Fénéon

Private Collection

Solemn silence
(left) In reality, the Sunday crowds were often rowdy and boisterous, but the people in Seurat's painting are dignified and restrained. He delights in showing the details of their clothes, their hats and canes, dainty fans and genteel reading-matter.

An empty landscape
Seurat made a detailed study of the landscape without any people in it.

Bridgeman Art Library

Whitney Collection, New York

Edimages-Palix

Art Institute of Chicago

The fashionable bustle
(above right) Seurat probably drew his elegant costumes from contemporary fashion-plates. The bustle was at the very height of fashion.

Sketches of monkeys
Seurat made four sheets of drawings for the monkey in the right foreground. In the painting he is spotted with yellow, purple and ultramarine.

Musée d'Orsay, Paris

Gallery

Seurat made over 20 outdoor studies for his first major painting, Bathing at Asnières, creating the finished picture in his studio. This exhaustive approach was typical of his working method, yet Seurat had not yet developed an individual technique. When he returned to the banks of the Seine to begin work on La Grande Jatte, he was in the

Bathing at Asnières *1883-84*
79″ × 118½″ National Gallery, London

This timeless image of working people relaxing at the weekend is set in the vicinity of the industrial suburb of Asnières. The air is heavy with the midsummer heat and the inhabitants have come to the island of La Grande Jatte to cool off by the banks of the Seine. In the background we see the railway bridge and the factory chimneys.

Men and boys in various stages of undress are spread out carefully through the landscape. Their simplified, static poses give the painting an air of silence and repose. Only the boy in the water, frozen in the act of cupping his hands to his mouth, seems to make any sound.

process of inventing an entirely new style of painting in tiny, brilliantly coloured dots.

During the summers, Seurat left Paris to paint many calm seascapes and quiet harbour views in his new style. He stayed in resorts like Grandcamp and Gravelines on the Normandy coast, hoping to 'freshen his eyes' after long bouts in the studio.

Back in the capital, Seurat found another rich source of subject matter in the lively night-life of Montmartre. His late masterpieces, La Parade, Le Chahut and The Circus (which he did not live to complete) all show entertainers of one kind or another – musicians, high-kicking dancers, graceful acrobats and clowns.

The Bec du Hoc, Grandcamp *1885*
26″ × 32½″ Tate Gallery, London

'Seurat's seascapes', wrote his friend Félix Fénéon, 'give off calm and melancholy. They ripple monotonously as far as the distant point where the sky comes down. One rock rules them tyrannically – the Bec du Hoc.' Here, the huge outcrop of rock juts across the canvas, dwarfing the distant sailing boats.

Boats at Grandcamp *1885*
25½″ × 32″ Private Collection, New York

*This tranquil seascape concentrates on the slim dark hulls and broad
white sails of boats passing along the seashore. A clump of intensely
coloured shrubbery – dotted with red, orange, purple and blue – fills
the centre of the composition. The sea itself is painted in Seurat's early
style, with small, controlled brushstrokes.*

La Grande Jatte *1884-86*
81″ × 120″ The Art Institute of
Chicago

In this vast painting Seurat portrays fashionable Parisians enjoying a lazy summer afternoon on the island of La Grande Jatte. Men and women stroll under the trees or recline on the river banks, watching the boaters on the Seine. In the foreground, an outrageously elegant couple walk a monkey on a leash. La Grande Jatte was never really as prim and proper as this, but as Seurat's first biographer remarked, the artist was 'too sedate to like the island as it really was'.

Bridgeman Art Library

GALLERY

La Parade *1888*
39¼″ × 59″ Metropolitan
Museum of Art, New York

Like many of his contemporaries, Toulouse-Lautrec among them, Seurat was fascinated by Parisian night-life: the café-concerts, the dance-halls and the circus. La Parade shows a carnival booth at the circus, illuminated by blazing gas-lamps. In the centre, the austere trombone-player stands out in dark silhouette. Behind him, the band in their derby hats dissolve in the brilliance of the stage-lighting. At the foot of the canvas, the heads of the inattentive audience look like cardboard cut-outs.

The Harbour at Gravelines *1890*
28¾″ × 36½″ Herron Art Institute, Indianapolis

Seurat spent the summer of 1890 at Gravelines, on the Channel coast, where he derived the inspiration for this peaceful harbour scene. He carefully composed the picture around the gentle curve of the sea wall, the sturdy bollard in the foreground and the slender masts of the boats at anchor. The cool clarity of the early morning light enhances the impression of absolute calm.

The Channel at Gravelines, Evening *1890*
25¾″ × 32¼″ From the Collection of Mr and Mrs William A. M. Burden

*The contrasting evening scene at Gravelines is one of Seurat's most
beautifully organized pictures. Horizontal strips of sand, shimmering
sea and sky create a mood of stillness and serenity. The dark anchors
silhouetted against the soft evening light serve as symbols of
restfulness and immobility, while their simple decorative shapes recall
the stylized forms of Japanese art.*

Le Chahut *1890*
67″ × 55¼″ Kröller-Müller Museum, Otterlo

In this nightclub scene, Seurat focuses our attention on the 'happy' diagonal lines formed by the dancers' raised legs as they perform 'Le Chahut', and the sloping neck of the double bass. The mood of gaiety is intensified by the leaping coat-tails of the male dancer and the 'smiling' bows on the women's shoes.

The Circus *1890-91*
73″ × 59″ Musée d'Orsay, Paris

*This lively circus scene was left unfinished at Seurat's death. Parts of
the design – the woman bare-back rider and the cheeky clown doing a
back flip – are based on circus posters of the period. The artist has
included a narrow, coloured border and constructed
a special frame, to complement the tones in the picture.*

Nights at the Circus

Like Degas and Toulouse-Lautrec before him, Seurat was a frequent visitor to the circus, which saw its heyday in Paris – and the rest of Europe – during the last years of the 19th century.

The permanent circuses set up in Europe during the second half of the 19th century brought together under one roof the many fairground acts which had provided amusement for centuries, including animal menageries, gymnasts, jugglers, conjurors and skilled horsemen. Acts good enough to attract and keep audiences could assure their performers of good salaries, status and fame – for circus acts toured around the continent, heralded by a blaze of advance publicity.

MIDGETS AND MERMAIDS

Success depended on astonishing the audience, and this the circuses did by exhibiting curiosities such as midgets, giants and 'mermaids'; training animals to perform tricks – such as elephants riding cycles; and inventing new and more

H. Roger Viollet

ingenious acrobatic acts, demanding faultless timing and relentless physical training on the part of the circus performers.

One act, which achieved tremendous notoriety in London after its first performance at Astley's Amphitheatre in 1864, was Mazeppa's Ride. A woman bareback rider named Adah Menken was strapped, supposedly naked (but in fact clothed in what now seems a quite decorous tunic), on the back of a 'wild' horse, which would then rear and gallop around the stage. The act had been performed for years, but never before by a woman.

It was the start of a new and immensely popular circus tradition of young female performers which introduced a risqué, slightly titillating aspect to the circus spectacular. Menken's daring ride was surpassed in 1877 when the young Madame Zazel (a girl from Leicester) was stuffed down the barrel

A show every night
(below) Paris boasted five permanent circuses during the 1880s. Housed in substantial buildings – like the Cirque d'Hiver, shown here after its conversion into a cinema – they featured action-packed shows every night of the week. The demand for sensational performances produced such incredible acts as the human cannonball and elephants riding bicycles.

J. Tissot/Amateur Circus/Museum of Fine Arts, Boston

Roger Viollet

The amateur circus
(left) The circus was so popular with all classes of society that wealthy amateurs produced their own shows. This painting by James Tissot shows two aristocratic trapeze artists.

The star of the show
The First Clown was billed as the leading performer even in the most spectacular circuses. He usually appeared between each act, teasing the audience with constant shifts from smiles to tears.

of a cannon – actually a spring-loaded catapult – and fired high above the audience at West's Amphitheatre in London. For each performance as a human cannonball, Madame Zazel received the then princely sum of £20, and retired with her fortune two years later.

ARTISTS AT THE CIRCUS

In France, as in England, the circuses vied with music-hall and cabaret as the most popular entertainment in the last decades of the century. Their success was such that in Paris there were five permanent circuses in the 1870s, each giving nightly performances. But the audiences they attracted were different from those in London, for these 'lowbrow' entertainments became a magnet for the artists and writers of the time. Circus acts

and individual performers were celebrated not just in the handbills and posters used for publicity, but in paintings that have since become world famous.

Painters and poets were attracted in particular to the Cirque Fernando in Montmartre, which opened in 1875. Being small, it had an intimacy not found in the larger Parisian circuses – certainly not in the rival Hippodrome, which was large enough to stage chariot races by the 1890s.

Performances at the Cirque Fernando were held at 8.30 each night in a circular wooden building, its high domed roof criss-crossed with brightly painted and gilded rafters. Seats rose steeply from the ring, allowing the audience a far greater sense of involvement and immediacy than in the huge big tops popular abroad. Every movement, every hesitation almost, could be seen.

The notorious Menken had performed

Both posters: Edimedia

Mazeppa's Ride here, and the circus still relied heavily on female horse-riding acts, controlled (as tradition demanded) by a moustachioed ringmaster, brandishing his whip. These female equestriennes would perform dance movements and somersaults bareback on a horse as it cantered round the ring. One, who doubled as a clown and also worked at the Moulin Rouge, was the curiously-named Cha-U-Kao who, along with the popular clowns Footit and Chocolat, was sketched and painted by Toulouse-Lautrec.

Daredevil feats were much in demand as always. A mulatto woman, Miss La La, helped to make the Cirque Fernando famous by an act in which, hanging by her teeth from a small iron ring, she would be hauled up to a high trapeze. By the 1880s and 90s young women had replaced men in many trapeze acts, sometimes performing without safety nets as an added thrill for the audience. Their graceful and perfectly-timed movements, inspired paintings by both Lautrec and Degas.

The Fernando was eventually renamed the Cirque Medrano, and moved to new premises, but its popularity as an artists' haunt lasted right into the 20th century. Picasso painted the acrobats and clowns he saw there and the writer Jean Cocteau was a frequent visitor. But although the circus put on shows right up to the 1950s, it declined in popularity after the first two decades of this century, overtaken by a new entertainment – the cinema.

BREATHTAKING FEATS

In their heyday, the circuses had spared no effort to keep one step ahead of the public, to whom what was sensational one day was old hat the next. To keep their audiences enthralled, performers provided ever greater thrills and breathtaking feats. In London and Paris there seemed no end to the risk artistes would take in order to draw the crowds.

In 1860, audiences flocked to the Cirque l'Impératrice in Paris to see an acrobat named Jules Léotard. He performed his trapeze act high over the ring, whizzing 20 feet through the air from one trapeze to another. Photographs of Léotard in mid-air, in 35 different poses, were being sold on the streets of Paris that summer, causing one observer to comment drily, 'In Paris, the man who risks his life, no matter how, whether or not it serves a useful purpose, is sure to start an infatuation.'

Léotard was quickly superseded in skill, as double and even triple back-somersaults in mid-air between trapezes became commonplace. But he did give his name to the bodystocking still worn for exercise and, in spite of his failure to cause any excitement among the blasé London audiences, he was the inspiration for the famous music-hall song 'That Daring Young Man on the Flying Trapeze'.

THE AMAZING BLONDIN

Léotard's success was soon eclipsed by that of Blondin, who in 1861 walked along a tightrope stretched 160 feet above Niagara Falls, carrying a man on his back and pausing in the middle to cook and eat an omelette. Blondin subsequently played to packed audiences at the Crystal Palace, where he would ascend to a great height by walking up a tightrope at a steep angle and performing various tricks once he reached the horizontal rope.

In terms of pure spectacle, little could rival

Chocolat and Footit
(right) Even nightclubs and music halls employed clowns during the 1890s. Chocolat and Footit appeared at the Moulin Rouge, where they were painted by Toulouse-Lautrec.

Traditional fun
(right) The main ingredients of circus entertainment have been standard fare for centuries: acrobats and jugglers, trapeze artists and clowns, performing horses and bareback riders. In this poster, the Paris Cirque Rancy advertises them all.

The bearded lady
Freak shows, featuring bearded ladies, mermaids, giants and dwarves, were a special attraction of the American circuses which visited Europe. But most were fakes, and looked convincing only from a distance.

Dangerous thrills
(right) In 1900, the lion tamer at the Hippodrome was badly mauled in the middle of his act, before a huge crowd. Competition between the circuses was so fierce that performers were forced to take ever-increasing risks to satisfy the public's thirst for dangerous acts.

Phineas T. Barnum's American Circus, performed in a huge, circular canvas tent which came to be known as the Big Top. Barnum was the first to dub his circus the 'Greatest Show on Earth' (now used by practically all circuses, however small) and in sheer size it certainly outstripped all its European counterparts. Barnum's circus, which opened in Brooklyn in 1871 and afterwards travelled to England, claimed to have 4,000 employees, performers and animals, with 32 acres of canvas, using three tons of sawdust at every venue.

THE ELDORADO ELF

The success of Barnum's gigantic show rested to a great extent on his own showmanship and skill at publicity. Among the attractions his circus boasted were exhibits that now seem altogether tasteless, but which Barnum knew the public would be agog to see, including Anna Leake, the Armless Woman; a troupe of 'man-eating cannibals' brought from Fiji; Admiral Dot, the Eldorado Elf; and Colonel Goshen, the Palestinian Giant. These were in addition to a large equestrian team, acrobats, conjurors, performing animals, an exotic menagerie, a waxworks and a full band.

Freaks – some of them genuine, but others depending on a large dose of gullibility and a certain physical distance on the part of the spectators – had been part of fairs for centuries and were still immensely popular. Barnum's world-famous circus – expanded in 1891 when he formed a partnership with James A. Bailey – exploited their appeal to the full. And Barnum & Bailey's Circus remained a byword in showbusiness history long after both founders had died, at the turn of the 20th century.

A Year in the Life 1885

Far from the endless summer of Seurat's Paris, French forces carried the flag of empire into Africa and China, while Britain's troops marched towards trouble in Khartoum. Help arrived too late to save General Gordon from the Mahdi, but there was happier news elsewhere: Louis Pasteur successfully treated rabies, and the Statue of Liberty was raised in New York harbour.

Gordon of Khartoum
The British General Charles Gordon (b.1833) was sent to Khartoum in 1884 to relieve an Egyptian garrison, and was besieged by Sudanese troops under their religious leader, the Mahdi. Gordon's urgent requests for help were answered too late. Two days before new troops arrived, on 26 January 1885, Gordon was killed and his head given to the Mahdi.

Edimedia

Georges W. Joy/Death of General Gordon/Private Collection

As Seurat was putting the finishing touches to his most famous pointillist painting *La Grande Jatte,* showing Parisians relaxing on a tranquil Sunday afternoon, the eyes of the French government were focused firmly overseas. The Prime Minister, Jules Ferry, had become a convinced colonialist.

THE FRENCH IN INDO-CHINA

France's grip on Madagascar, where Britain was her chief rival, was soon strengthened and the exploration of Brazza in the Congo was pursued so effectively that the International Congress of colonial nations gave formal recognition to the creation of the French Congo. But France's attempt to recover Tonkin in Annam (now Vietnam) led to undeclared war with China. On Sunday, 29 March, thousands of Parisians were disturbed by the arrival of newspaper boys shouting 'Retreat of the French Troops! Invasion of Tonkin by the Chinese.'

A despatch received from General Brière d'Isle had announced the defeat of a French army. When the Chamber of Deputies assembled on the Monday, the news of this relatively minor reverse – and Ferry's appeal for a credit of 200 million francs to pay for reinforcements – roused the fury of the government's anti-colonialist enemies. The debate was bitter: the radical leader Clemenceau accused Ferry of high treason and the crowds shouted for the death of 'Ferry Tonkin'.

The Government was overthrown, but Ferry had secret information that China was prepared to accept French suzerainty in Annam. Despite opposition, the French presence

Mary Evans Picture Library

The Arabian Nights

The most famous English translation of The Arabian Nights, *by Sir Richard Burton, was published in 1885. In the book, Queen Sheherazade keeps her husband from killing her by beginning a story every night and promising to finish it the next one. The stories, including* Aladdin, Ali Baba *and* Sinbad the Sailor *– illustrated here – are so popular that they have become part of Western folklore.*

LÉOPOLD II

BRUXELLES

Edimages

Peter Newark's Western Americana

Golf reaches America

Joseph Mickle Fox of Philadelphia introduced the game of golf to the United States in 1885, later forming the Foxburg Golf Club, the oldest in the country. He learnt the game in Scotland, probably at St Andrews – shown here – and brought back with him the first left-handed clubs and some gutty balls.

King Leopold's Congo

In 1885, the Congo in central Africa became the sovereign possession of Leopold II, King of the Belgians. At first he declared it a free-trade zone, but during the next 20 years his personal forces colonized the vast country, and monopolized trade in rubber and ivory. Control was transferred to the Belgian state in 1908.

in Indo-China was there to stay. And in fact the credits the Chamber had refused to Ferry were soon granted to his successor, M. Brisson.

Another imperial crisis, this time in the Egyptian-ruled Sudan, contributed to the overthrow of Gladstone's Liberal government in England. Two years earlier, under their religious leader, the Mahdi, Sudanese warriors had risen against the Egyptians and utterly destroyed a force sent in by the Egyptian Khedive commanded by the British. Public opinion at home, led by Queen Victoria, had been outraged at this blow to British prestige. In January 1884, after much reluctance, Gladstone had been persuaded to send out the evangelical General Gordon to deal with the situation.

When he reached Khartoum, Gordon asked for troops to keep open the Nile route out of the Sudan. Gladstone hesitated: he dreaded the idea of another colonial intervention and warned the House of Commons that an attack on the Mahdi would be 'a war against people struggling to be free'. Finally he gave way, and in October 1884 a grant of £300,000 financed a relief expedition of 10,000 men ready to advance up the Nile from Cairo under Lord Wolseley.

GORDON'S DEATH

But it arrived too late. The expedition took three months to fight along the 1,000 miles of river and when the advance party arrived at Khartoum, it was confronted by the news that the town had fallen to the Mahdi two days before. Gordon had

Archiv für Kunst und Geschichte

Peter Newark's Western Americana

Jumbo the Elephant
Jumbo was the greatest attraction at Barnum's circus. But tragedy struck on 15 September 1885, when the animals were boarding the circus train. Jumbo was the last to cross the line, and a passing train knocked him down. He died soon afterwards.

Mary Evans Picture Library

136

been killed. His head had been cut off and taken to the Mahdi.

When the news of Gordon's death reached England, a wave of hysteria erupted. Gladstone was hissed and booed. The crowds in Downing Street no longer called him G.O.M. (Grand Old Man) but M.O.G. (Murderer of Gordon). Queen Victoria sent a telegram blaming Gladstone for the delay in sending out a relief force, and even ordered that the telegram should not be sent in cypher, so that officials could read of her displeasure with her Prime Minister. On 12 March, Parliament voted Gordon's family a grant of £20,000 and the next day was declared a national day of mourning for the hero of Khartoum, with services at St Paul's Cathedral and Westminster Abbey.

It was, however, events in Afghanistan which enabled the British government to extricate themselves from the Sudan. On 30 March, the Russians attacked the Afghans at Penjdeh on the northern frontier of Afghanistan. They calculated that Britain was too enmeshed in the Sudan to react, but the British press and public opinion were quick to perceive the danger to India. On 27 April Gladstone pledged that troops from the Sudan would be used to meet the new threat. Thus he was able to extricate Britain from further commitment in the Sudan, while his resolute stand forced the Russians to negotiate.

GLADSTONE FALLS

But Gladstone's problems were far from solved. On 8 June the government was defeated over its budget proposals. The Marquis of Salisbury was summoned to Queen Victoria and

The price of Niagara
(left) The Niagara Falls, which form part of the boundary between the United States and Canada, were sold to New York State in 1885 for $1,500,000. The river Niagara drops more than 150ft over two falls.

Statue of Liberty
The Statue of Liberty arrived in New York in 1885, a gift from France to the United States to commemorate their friendship. It stands 305ft high, with an observation platform in the head giving a magnificent view of New York harbour.

Jean-Loup Charmet

Death of Ulysses S. Grant
(left) Ulysses S. Grant (1822-85) earned glory as a victorious general in the American Civil War. In 1869, he became Republican President of the USA at a time when bribery and corruption were rife. But Grant's reputation did not suffer. He died a respected man.

The Canadian-Pacific Railway
(right) The railway from the St Lawrence River in eastern Canada to the Pacific Coast in the west was completed in 1885, and helped unify the country. Rail links with the United States soon followed.

Peter Newark's Western Americana

137

invited to form a new Conservative caretaker government. This staggered on until a general election in December.

During the summer, while in opposition, Gladstone came to a momentous decision – he must come out for Irish Home Rule. He wanted time to educate his party in this new way of thinking, but this he did not get, for after the general election in December, the Irish Nationalists held the balance of power in Parliament. Whoever they supported, Liberal or Conservative, would rule Britain. Gladstone's son, Herbert, announced his father's change of mind to several London newspaper editors, and when the news hit the headlines Salisbury's government was doomed. Gladstone returned to power.

Away from politics, the British had a royal event to celebrate when on 23 July, Queen Victoria's youngest daughter, Princess Beatrice, was married to Prince Henry of Battenburg. The wedding took place on the Isle of Wight and the reception was held in brilliant sunshine on the lawns of Osborne House, the Queen's favourite residence.

The dramatic year had seen many innovations. Gladstone had created the first Jewish peer in Britain, Sir Nathaniel Rothschild. In France, Louis Pasteur had demonstrated the effectiveness of his rabies vaccine by successfully treating Joseph Meister. In America, the Washington monument had been dedicated on 21 February, and the 555ft-tall white marble obelisk was the highest structure in the land even after the arrival in May of a gift from the French – Bartholdi's female figure of 'Liberty Enlightening the World', better known as the Statue of Liberty, which stands today in New York harbour.

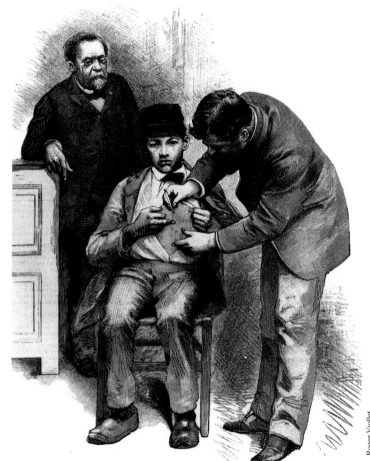

Anna Pavlova
Anna Pavlova, the famous Russian ballerina, was born in 1885. She began her career with the Russian Imperial Ballet in St Petersburg, then went on to join Diaghilev's company for his first Paris season. Later she formed her own company and embarked on a series of world tours, bringing ballet to countries that had never seen it before. She died in 1931.

Pasteur's rabies vaccine
In 1885, a peasant boy severely bitten by a rabid dog was treated with a vaccine by Louis Pasteur. The boy survived and others came for treatment; soon vaccination against rabies became routine throughout the world, and deaths caused by the virus dropped dramatically.

GALLERY GUIDE

Cézanne
Overall, the best selection of Cézanne's pictures is in Paris. The Musée d'Orsay contains several very fine still-lifes and landscapes, while the Orangerie can boast of the excellent *Nymphs by the Sea* series, the forerunners of *The Great Bathers*. The most famous version of the latter is in the Philadelphia Museum of Art (p.32), which also owns one of the artist's many depictions of his wife. Further examples of Cézanne's portrait style can be seen in New York, Boston and Washington. The artist is well-represented in London, too, at the Courtauld Institute Galleries, which possess a number of landscapes (pp.19, 29), *The Card Players* (pp.26-7) and the virtuoso *Still-life with Plaster Cupid*.

Gauguin
Gauguin is particularly well-represented in American collections: the Museum of Fine Arts, Boston, the Metropolitan Museum of Art, New York (p.65), the Art Institute, Chicago (p.52), and the Albright-Knox Art Gallery, Buffalo (pp.50-51). The latter also houses a fine example of Gauguin's Breton work (p.57), although the most celebrated picture from this period is in the Walter P. Chrysler Jr. Collection, New York *(Loss of Virginity)*. In Europe, the best selections of Gauguin's earlier style can be seen in Paris and in Copenhagen. In Britain, two of Gauguin's most mysterious Tahitian scenes can be found in the Courtauld Institute Galleries *(Nevermore* and *The Dream)*, while the National Gallery of Scotland owns the painting which made his reputation (p.56). Other works can be found in Russia, most notably in the Pushkin Museum, Moscow and in the Hermitage, Leningrad.

Van Gogh
The best collections of Van Gogh's work are in his native Holland, at the Kröller-Müller Museum, Otterlo, and at the National Museum Vincent Van Gogh, Amsterdam. The former is particularly strong in examples of his early, naturalistic style. There are fine portraits at the Musée d'Orsay, Paris, and at the Courtauld Institute Galleries, London, while the National Gallery, London, contains a superb example of the artist's late landscape style. In America, Van Gogh's best-known works are at the Museum of Modern Art, New York *(Starry Night*, pp.94-5) and at the Metropolitan Museum of Art (one of the versions of *Sunflowers*), while the Yale University Art Gallery possesses *The Night Café*.

Seurat
The brevity of Seurat's career, combined with his painstaking approach, allowed him to complete comparatively few major works in his fully developed, Pointillist style. The most important of these is certainly *La Grande Jatte* (pp.122-3, Art Institute, Chicago) and Seurat is also well-represented in New York, where the Metropolitan Museum of Art owns *La Parade* and the atmospheric *Evening at Honfleur*. Further examples of the artist's coastal scenes can be seen in St Louis, Detroit and Minneapolis (p.115), while the Norton Simon Foundation, Los Angeles, owns one of the finest of his early depictions of labourers. In Paris, the Musée d'Orsay possesses *The Circus* (p.129) and the best single collection of Seurat's remarkable chalk drawings while, in London, there are major works at the National Gallery and the Courtauld Institute Galleries.

BIBLIOGRAPHY

G. Boudaille, *Gauguin*, Thames and Hudson, London, 1964

A. Bowness, *Post-Impressionism*, Weidenfeld and Nicolson, London, 1980

Van Wyck Brooks (translator), *Paul Gauguin's Intimate Journals*, Indiana University Press, Bloomington, 1958

P. Cabanne, *Van Gogh*, Thames and Hudson, New York, 1986

P. Courthion, *Seurat*, Abrams, New York, 1968

I. Dunlop, *The Complete Paintings of Cézanne*, Penguin, New York, 1986

R. Fry and A. Blunt, *Seurat*, Phaidon, Oxford, 1965

W. Homer, *Seurat and the Science of Painting*, M.I.T. Press, Cambridge, 1964

R. Murphy, *The World of Cézanne*, Time-Life Books, Alexandria, 1968

J. Rewald, *Cézanne*, Abrams, New York, 1986

J. Rewald, *Post-Impressionism from Van Gogh to Gauguin*, Museum of Modern Art, New York, 1956

J. Russell, *Seurat*, Thames and Hudson, New York, 1985

R. Wallace, *The World of Van Gogh*, Time-Life Books, Alexandria, 1969

Louis Anquetin (1861-1932)

French painter; with Bernard, one of the pioneers of Cloisonnisme. Anquetin was born in Normandy but trained in Paris, initially with the academic painter, Bonnat, and then at the Atelier Cormon, where he befriended Van Gogh and Bernard. Anquetin flirted briefly with Divisionism, but rapidly rejected it in favour of the new Cloisonnist style which he developed with Bernard. This blend of elements from Japanese prints, stained-glass windows and enamelwork formed the basis of Bernard's Synthetism and was ultimately to influence Gauguin. Anquetin's greatest achievement in this vein was the superb Street – Five O'Clock in the Evening, *(1887), which can be seen at the Wadsworth Athenaeum, Hartford, Connecticut.*

Emile Bernard (1868-1941)

French Synthetist painter, whose work exerted a profound influence on Gauguin. Bernard attended Cormon's studio in 1885. There, he met Anquetin, Van Gogh and Toulouse Lautrec, before being expelled for insubordinate behaviour. He toyed with Pointillism, until an argument with Signac caused him to destroy his canvases in this style. Subsequently, he and Anquetin developed the Cloisonnist technique, which laid the foundations for his own pictorial symbolism. Bernard showed the resulting Synthetist paintings to Gauguin, during a stay at Pont Aven, and these prompted the latter to produce his Vision after the Sermon *(p.56). Bernard was later to feel much aggrieved that Gauguin had taken all the credit for these innovations. His own career was interrupted by lengthy travels, which included an eleven-year stay in Cairo. On his return to France, Bernard was drawn to the art of Cézanne and, in 1905, he instituted the 'Aesthetic Revival' movement.*

The intimacies of everyday life
(below) Instead of the more usual landscape subjects painted by the Impressionists, Intimist painters like Bonnard preferred to depict the minutiae of domestic life. Nude in the Bath *is a typical example.*

Lauros-Giraudon

Petit Palais, Paris/SPADEM © 1988

Pierre Bonnard (1867-1947)

French Intimist painter and co-founder of the Nabis. Bonnard trained at the Ecole des Beaux-Arts and at the Académie Julian, where he met other members of the Nabis. Like them, he was committed to the development of the applied arts and, in this respect, he followed the example of Gauguin and Japanese prints. However, Bonnard did not share the group's general leaning towards Symbolism and, both in his subject matter and in his treatment of light, he was · closer to the Impressionists. He shared a studio with Vuillard and, like him, preferred to depict the typically Intimist themes of everyday, domestic scenes.

Henri Edmond Cross (Henri Delacroix) (1856-1910)

One of the principal Neo-Impressionist painters. Originally from Douai, Cross (he anglicized his name from Delacroix) studied in Paris under Bonvin and exhibited with the Impressionists at the Salon des Indépendants. He adopted the pointillist technique comparatively late, in 1891, the year in which he settled on the Mediterranean coast. There, he embarked on a series of idyllic landscapes, depicting female bathers by sun-drenched shores. These were an important influence on the young Matisse, who visited Cross in 1904.

Maurice Denis (1870-1943)

Important Symbolist painter; a founder of the Nabis. Denis studied at the Lycée Condorcet, where he met Vuillard and Roussel, before coming into contact with the remainder of the Nabis at the Académie Julian. Denis was a founder member of the group in 1888 and his article, The Definition of Neo-Traditionalism *(1890), is the most significant document relating to the group's activities. As the title suggests, Denis looked to the past for inspiration – in his case, early Italian art – and this resulted in a highly decorative, linear style. He shared the other Nabis' interest in the applied arts and this led him to produce, among other things, stained-glass designs, stage scenery and book illustrations. He was also a devout Catholic and, in 1903, he accompanied Sérusier to the art centre at the German monastery of Beuron. Accordingly, much of his later career was devoted to religious painting.*

Charles Filiger (1863-1928)

French religious painter, working mainly in Brittany. Filiger was born in Alsace and studied in Paris, at the Atelier Colorassi. In 1889, he moved to Le Pouldu in Brittany, where he became friendly with Gauguin, Bernard and the Nabis. Despite these contacts, Filiger remained a very independent artist and his best-known works, the strange series of circular pictures which he called Chromatic Notations, *resembled Byzantine icons executed in a primitive, pointillist technique. Filiger exhibited at the first Rose + Croix Salon in 1892,* but became increasingly reclusive as he grew older. In 1905, he was adopted by a Breton family, who cared for him until he committed suicide in 1928.

Georges Lacombe (1868-1916)
French painter and sculptor, a member of the Nabis. Lacombe came from a wealthy background and studied both at the Roll studio and at the Académie Julian. He spent his summers at an artist's colony at Camaret in Brittany and, in 1892, he met Sérusier, who invited him to join the Nabis. His exhibits for the group included striking seascapes and decorative Breton scenes that owed much to both Sérusier and Gauguin. The latter was also a major influence on Lacombe's wood carvings, which exuded a raw, primitive energy, comparable to that of Polynesian sculpture. Lacombe eventually settled in Normandy and turned increasingly to landscape subjects. However, traces of Symbolism remained and his strongest later work was Femmes Damnées, a series of bas-reliefs illustrating a poem by Baudelaire.

Maximilien Luce (1858-1941)
French Neo-Impressionist painter. Luce was trained as a wood engraver, but is better known for the pointillist paintings which he produced after 1887, when he met Seurat and Signac. Initially, he worked on rather schematic landscapes and coastal scenes but, in the 1890s, his visits to the Belgian poet, Verhaeren, led him to depict industrial subjects. Luce had anarchist sympathies and he was imprisoned in 1894.

Théo van Rysselberghe (1862-1926)
Belgian painter and decorative artist, active both in Paris and Brussels. Rysselberghe was born in Ghent and studied both there and in Brussels. In 1883, he was a co-founder of Les Vingt, an important exhibiting body, which provided an international forum for avant-garde artistic trends. Les Vingt was particularly influential in the development of Symbolism and Neo-Impressionism, and the latter transformed Rysselberghe's style, after Seurat and Signac had exhibited in Brussels. He became one of the most loyal practitioners of Pointillism – continuing to employ it until about 1910 and extending its range to include portraiture and genre painting. In 1897, he moved to Paris, where he provided a useful point of contact between the two capitals.

Paul Sérusier (1863-1927)
Co-founder and leader of the Nabis. Sérusier came from a wealthy commercial family and worked initially at a papermill. In 1888, he turned to painting, training at the Académie Julian, where he met Denis, Ranson and Bonnard. In the same year, he met Gauguin at Pont Aven and, under his instruction, produced The Talisman, a key-work, which took Symbolist painting to the brink of abstraction. This picture, and the new aesthetic which accompanied it, were also the stimuli which prompted Sérusier and his friends at the Académie Julian to found the Nabis. Sérusier was one of the least talented artists in this group, but his thorough grasp of aesthetics enabled him to promote its artistic direction. His conviction that painting needed a firm spiritual basis was fired by his visit to the Benedictine monastery of Beuron, where he discovered the art of the German Primitives. This helped him to formulate his own theories, which he expounded in The ABC of Painting (1921).

Paul Signac (1863-1935)
After Seurat, the leading Neo-Impressionist artist. Signac's early style was influenced by Monet and the Impressionists, and he became a founder member of the Society of Independent Artists. Through this, he met Seurat and, in 1886, he exhibited pointillist paintings at the final Impressionist show. Signac was firmly convinced of the superiority of the divisionist technique and his book, From Eugène Delacroix to Neo-Impressionism (1899), was, effectively, the manifesto of the movement. He settled in the South of France in 1892 and was a formative influence on Matisse.

Felix Vallotton (1865-1925)
Swiss artist, associated with the Nabis. Vallotton arrived in Paris in 1882, where he studied at the Ecole des Beaux-Arts and the Académie Julian. His earliest work was in the Realist tradition, but the important exhibition of Japanese art in 1890 prompted him towards a simpler, stylized approach and resulted in the superb series of woodcuts which he produced throughout the 1890s. Vallotton exhibited with both the Rosicrucians and the Nabis. He was closest to Vuillard, sharing his gift for imparting an air of mystery into domestic interiors.

Edouard Vuillard (1868-1940)
French Intimist painter, the greatest of the Nabis. Vuillard studied under Gérôme and then at the Académie Julian, where he came into contact with members of the Nabis. Like Bonnard, Vuillard excelled at the depiction of intimate, domestic scenes. However, by fusing his hunched figures with the patterns of their backgrounds, he brought to these interiors a closed, hermetic quality.

Archiv für Kunst und Geschichte/DACS 1988

Albi Museum

The Nabis
(left) Like Bonnard, Lacombe, Denis and Sérusier, Edouard Vuillard was a member of the Nabis. In his portrait of his friend, Toulouse-Lautrec, Vuillard uses the large areas of flat colour that were one of the main features of the Nabis' revolt against Impressionism.

INDEX